JOHN DOBSON
Architect & Landscape
Gardener

BY THE SAME AUTHOR

Tyneside Classical (With Gordon Dodds)
Tyneside Portraits

JOHN DOBSON 1787 – 1865

JOHN DOBSON

Architect & Landscape Gardener

by

Lyall Wilkes

ORIEL PRESS

STOCKSFIELD

BOSTON   HENLEY   LONDON

First published in 1980
by Oriel Press Ltd. (Routledge & Kegan Paul Ltd.)
Branch End, Stocksfield,
Northumberland, NE43 7 NA

Printed in Great Britain
by Knight & Forster Ltd., Leeds

ISBN 0 85362 181 0

For My Wife
MARGARET

CONTENTS

INTRODUCTION

JOHN DOBSON, according to his daughter Margaret Jane, "had the fastidiousness of a retiring nature", and in her *Memoir* published in 1885 she lamented that "Many architects keep careful catalogues of their work for future reference but my father had neglected to do this—and left no notes or memorandum". Robin Gard, Northumberland County Archivist writes – "Considering the tremendous number of houses he built, or had a hand in, it seems almost incredible to me that there is so little". Moreover Dobson's letters to and from the members of the Smirke family are apparently lost as are the letters to and from other London friends such as John Varley, Turner, Hunt, Mulready and Benjamin West.

Fortunately sufficient in the way of sketch books, documents, letters, plans and drawings have come to light during the preparation of this book to bring Dobson out of the shadows as a human being; and like a great many artists his work now speaks for him. This is the first book devoted to Dobson, and only now—a hundred and fifteen years after his death—is appreciation of his work and status growing. Gervase Jackson-Stops in an article on Dobson's work in Country Life[1] described him as, "one of the most accomplished architects ever to have practised outside London—Dobson was in no way a provincial and his work is consistently more interesting and more accomplished than many of his better known contemporaries".

Without co-operation from the owners of Dobson houses this book would have been impossible. To Brigadier and Mrs Mitford of Mitford Hall, to Mr Philip Riddell of Cheesburn Grange, to Mr Aidan Cuthbert of Beaufront Castle, to Mr John Cookson of Meldon Park, to Mr and Mrs Duncan Davidson of Lilburn Tower and to Mrs Duncan of Prestwick Lodge my thanks are due for their help and hospitality, their readiness to answer questions and for permission to reproduce photographs of the beautiful interiors of their homes. To Mr Bruce Allsopp, formerly Reader in the History of Architecture at the University of Newcastle upon Tyne I am grateful for wise advice and suggestions. I am further indebted to him for drawing to my attention Dobson's sketch plans in the Newcastle University Library for the proposed Classical Church of St. John which was to have been built in Elswick, but unfortunately never was, and I am obliged to the University of Newcastle and to the Chief Librarian Dr. Enright for permission to reproduce some of the drawings. To Mr Peter Elphick FRIBA my thanks are due for helping me to find other Dobson material. Mr Robin Gard provided me with Dobson's letters to his lawyer Percival Fenwick of Prestwick Lodge, Ponteland concerning the quarrel with Grainger which ended their professional relationship. To Sir Stephen Middleton who found me the rare photograph of Sir Charles Monck, and to Mr Greg, Deputy Director of the Laing Art Gallery who allowed me to reproduce some of the drawings from Dobson's Sketch Book in the Gallery's possession, as well as allowing me to reproduce some Dobson watercolours from their collection, I am most grateful.

To Mr Howard Colvin of St. John's College, Oxford I am obliged for criticism of my list and my dating of Dobson's attributed work. Any errors in this list (and there must be several) are mine alone.

I thank the officers of the Northern Region of the Royal Institute of British Architects (formerly the Northern Architectural Association) for allowing me to examine the Proceedings and Minutes of the meetings of the Association since 1859, their founding year, and also the officers of the Whitby Literary and Philosophical Society for their assistance. To Mr Roy Angell, Newcastle upon Tyne City Planning Officer, I am obliged for answering queries about the present state of some of Dobson's buildings. Dr. C. I. C. Bosanquet has established beyond doubt that Dobson's alterations to Rock Hall were not done in 1845, as was stated in Dobson's daughter's list, but shortly after 1819. Innumerable other owners and ex-owners of Dobson houses have helped me with a date or attribution and I hope they will forgive me if there is not space to list all their names.

The captions on the photographs make clear the debt I owe to *Country Life* for permission to use photographs taken by their photographers.

John Dobson

CHAPTER ONE

EARLY DAYS AND ACHIEVEMENTS

In 1811 John Dobson, at the age of twenty-four, returned to Newcastle to practise as an architect after a year in London studying under the watercolourist John Varley. He was fortunate in that apart from Ignatius Bonomi[2] in County Durham, he was the only practising architect between York and Edinburgh. Yet as Dobson wryly said later[3] "Like myself he had little or no practise".

Dobson began to practise at a time when the architect was struggling to emerge as a member of a learned profession distinct from builders and masons. These builders and masons under the direction of a landed aristocracy of taste who knew exactly what they wanted, had built so successfully as to make the emergence of the professional architect appear unnecessary. An architect addressing the Northern Architectural Association on 11th May 1860 said that his architect father had often heard builders boast that in their area, "No architect could live; they made the place too hot for them".

At the beginning of the 19th century builders carried out the designs made by or ordered by their aristocratic patrons. But some of these builders made their own designs and executed them, and some presumed to call themselves architects. But of course there was no governing body, no examinations, no Institute of British Architects until 1835; and since anyone (including Richard Grainger) could call themselves architect, the separation of the designing from the building function itself was slow to develop.

Long after 1835 it was a common complaint of architects that after a year or so in an architect's office, a builder's son would rejoin his father's building business with a trade card proclaiming "designs neatly executed", and was only too ready to explain to his father's clients how easily the fees charged by architects could be avoided, because *his* designs would not be charged for.

What sustained the new profession was the growth of a new class

1

grown rich on coal, iron and commerce, which wanted to build in a way that reflected their new wealth and aspirations, but who lacked the taste and confidence of the landed aristocracy and so needed the architect rather than the mason.

Margaret Jane Dobson in the *Memoir* of her father published in 1885 stressed the difficulties facing Dobson at the beginning of his career—"Surrounded as we now are by architects it is difficult to realise what little employment there was for them at that time. In point of fact there were no architects then in the North of England in the strict sense of the word. Such buildings as were required were designed by builders only. Some of these fortunately were men of talent as the elegant proportions of the Tower of All Saints Church, Newcastle, designed and built by Mr. David Stephenson, clearly testify. Mr. Newton, another builder, designed the Assembly Rooms,[4] Newcastle".

It is not known beyond doubt which was Dobson's first building. McKenzie in his History of Newcastle[5] (published in 1827) states that the Royal Jubilee School, "a noble chaste and substantial building", then next to the Keelmen's Hospital in City Road was built between 1810 and 1811 from John Dobson's design. If this is true, this must be Dobson's first building. It is long since demolished, but was certainly as classical a work as Dobson ever designed. Dobson clearly had affection for it, for he made a watercolour of it which is in the Laing Art Gallery, and it is listed by H.M. Colvin who gives McKenzie as his authority. It was also listed as a Dobson building in the obituary notice printed in the Newcastle Daily Chronicle on 9th January 1865. But it is not listed in Margaret Jane Dobson's list of her father's buildings who gives the date of her father's first building as 1813 (North Seaton Hall). Much may be said of the inaccuracy of Miss Dobson's list, but the inaccuracy consists usually of claiming non-Dobson work as Dobson's, rather than in omission. It is also difficult to believe that Dobson did not tell his daughter with some pride which was his first building, and if this important building really was his first he would have been particularly likely to mention it.

Moreover the design is stated by McKenzie to have been in existence on 23rd March 1810 at the first meeting of the school's subscribers. Yet this was before Dobson left Newcastle for London in 1810. So if this building was Dobson's, it presupposes that an important building then costing £2194, and built to celebrate the jubilee of King George III was commissioned from Dobson when he was still a pupil under David

2

Photograph of Sir Charles Monck
1779 – 1867
(by courtesy of Sir Stephen Middleton, Bart)

The Young Dobson
(From a painting in the Laing Art Gallery collection)

Watercolour by Dobson of Royal Jubilee School, Newcastle upon Tyne
1810 – 1811
Possibly Dobson's first building?
(Laing Art Gallery)

In the Greek fashion, The Moot Hall
Newcastle upon Tyne by William Stokoe, 1812
(*Ursula Clark*)

4

Stephenson or at least before he commenced to practise. This seems so unlikely as to lead one to distrust McKenzie's attribution, even although his book was published only seventeen years after the school was built. If the building is not by Dobson it is most possibly by Stokoe who designed and built Newcastle's Grecian Moot Hall, also in 1810–1812.

The most important event in Dobson's first year or so in Newcastle (1811), after his return from his year in London, was his meeting and friendship with Sir Charles Monck (he had changed his name from Middleton), a passionate devotee of Grecian art and architecture who had returned from a prolonged Grecian honeymoon determined to build himself a new Mansion at Belsay to the strictest Grecian design. Monck was under the influence not only of things Grecian, but of his friend the redoubtable Sir William Gell, classicist, archaeologist, dilettante, author of several works of Classical topography and of 800 drawings in the British Museum and who in 1814 accompanied the Princess Caroline to Greece as one of her Chamberlains.

Sir Charles Monck although a highly individual man was a man of his time at least in his devotion to Greek architecture. From about 1616, when the Queen's House at Greenwich was designed (two years after Jones' last visit to Rome), classical architecture based upon Roman forms reinterpreted by Palladio became dominant in England. The most influental English interpreters of Palladio and Comassio were Inigo Jones, Wren and Lord Burlington. By the middle of the 18th Century the classical architecture of the Georgians was in danger of being restricted by the conventions of the previous hundred and fifty years—a beautiful strait jacket, but a strait jacket none the less.

It was broken by the new enthusiasm for, and the new freedom given by the rediscovery of an architecture even earlier than the Roman—the Greek. The Grand Tour was now more adventurous and frequently included Greece. Archaeologists were not only digging up Grecian works of art but uncovering measuring and recording Greek temples. From 1738 the recovery of Greek works of art from Pompeii and Herculaeum had aroused much public curiosity. It was the rediscovery of Europe's earliest classical inheritance. In 1762 two architects, James Stuart and Nicholas Revett (designer of the Grecian Church at Ayot St. Lawrence) began the publication of *The Antiquities of Athens*, and during the next fifty years or so Grecian (or designs which were thought to be Grecian) became High Fashion—hence such varied manifestations of the

5

new taste in Wedgwood, the loose flowing gowns in fashionable wardrobes and Keats' *Ode on a Grecian Urn*. Sir Charles like his friend Sir William Gell, had been an antiquarian from his youth and caught the fever early.

Few architects were completely unaffected by this English-Grecian interpretation of European neo-Classicism but its influence was particularly potent in the work of W. and H. W. Inwood whose St. Pancras Church in London is one of the most accomplished of neo-Greek designs, Decimus Burton, architect of The Athenaeum, Sir John Soane of The Bank of England, Sir Robert Smirke of The British Museum and John Dobson.

But along with scholarship and purity of style there was a growing taste for eclecticism, not only in the sense of choosing among a variety of styles but increasingly in that combination of chosen elements from different styles which was to become so characteristic of much mid-Victorian Architecture. Robert Adam (d. 1792) had already mingled styles and drawn impartially from Greek and Roman models, as at Syon House, Kedleston Hall and the library at Kenwood. So had James Wyatt, but the leaders of neo-Classicism in Britain (and Edinburgh played an important role) generally preferred to work in a simple, supposedly pure style, though they would switch from Greek to Gothic according to the requirements and taste of their client and not infrequently chose Gothic in deference to the scenic qualities of a site.

Romanticism flourished along with Classicism. The study of Latin and Greek were basic in the education given by the grammar schools and public schools, as well as the universities, and classical allusions became a convention in parliamentary speeches to the point of absurdity, while in architecture the tension between Classical formality and Romantic emotion reflected the cultural dichotomy of the late eighteenth and early nineteenth centuries.

But whether buildings were Classical or Gothic decorative effect predominated over functional considerations. Pillars rarely took the real weight of the building and even within the Gothic idiom the plan and massing might remain basically Palladian. The tension between symmetry and emotion, between proportion and romanticism, could be restrained within classical temple forms and were held there until the 1840's. It is interesting to note that the neo-Greek movement had moral and libertarian overtones associated with Athenian democracy and much

Belsay Hall, the Atrium by Sir Charles Monck
John Dobson drew the Ionic capitals for him
(*From* Historic Architecture of Northumberland and Newcastle upon Tyne *by*
Bruce Allsopp and Ursula Clark)

7

The Grecian taste in decoration, a cornice by Dobson at Mitford Hall
(*Ken Hitcham, Philipson Studios*)

influenced by Lord Byron. There was felt to be a certain *virtue* in the Greek style which was appropriate for public buildings and extended from great country houses to the cottages and lodges associated with them, as at Belsay in Northumberland. The caryatid, the anthemion, acanthus leaves, deep cornices of Grecian type and string courses enriched with Greek key pattern had emotional appeal to rival the romanticism of neo-Gothic.

When exactly Dobson met Sir Charles we do not know, but that Dobson from some uncertain date assisted Sir Charles in the design of parts of Belsay Hall, which was begun in 1810, is clear from the extract from a notebook[6] belonging to Sir Stephen Middleton— 'Sir Charles had a difficulty in getting the Ionic capitals cut from the drawings—Dobson the architect modelled one in clay or made a plaster cast for the masons to work from. Dobson also drew the capitals of the Doric columns in the Portico, the curve is a hyperbola'. There is an interesting later extract from the same notebook—'Having no precedent for windows in Greek Architecture he (Monck) decided to make them quite plain with no moulding round them. Dobson approved this and adopted it in Grey and Grainger Streets, Newcastle'.

More important to Dobson than this work in a subordinate capacity to Monck was the introduction it provided to Monck's Northumbrian friends; for Monck's enthusiasm for things Grecian set a fashion in Northumberland, and Belsay itself created a sensation.[7] The influence and work of Monck has been underestimated. Time and again one sees in Northumberland some classical decoration or improvement superimposed on an older house such as Preston Tower which might be Dobson's work. In the absence of plans and original documents this can only be speculation, but it seems very probable that some of the gentry seeing Belsay, decided to refashion at least the exteriors of their houses to make them more fashionable, drew their own designs (or got Monck to assist them) and used their own estate craftsman. Linden Hall, a house until recently thought to be pure Dobson and attributed to him, has recently been discovered by Mr. Bruce Allsopp to be by Monck. Had the now known date of Linden (1812) been known previously, more hesitation in the attribution to Dobson might have been shown, since so important and large a commission would not readily have been given to a young architect in the first year or so of his practice.

John Dobson was born on 9th December 1787 in the building which is now the Pineapple Inn in High Chirton, North Shields. As a young child he showed an exceptional gift for drawing and his father, a Nurseryman and Gardener on a considerable scale, at Chirton, and plainly a man of sensibility, gave the boy every opportunity to develop his talent. Dobson always acknowledged "having in youth the advantage of seeing the practical part of planting and gardening from my late father", and all his life described himself as an "Architect and Landscape Gardener".

At the age of fifteen he became a pupil-clerk with David Stephenson, the leading designer-builder in Newcastle, builder of the exquisite circular Church of All Saints, designed by him in the Wren Restoration style. Stephenson had also designed between 1784 and 1789 the new Mosley Street connecting the St. Nicholas Church area with Pilgrim Street, and built the small and very attractive Theatre Royal near Drury Lane at the bottom of what was later to be Grey Street.

This theatre was demolished in 1834 by Grainger in the building of Upper Dene Street (later to be called Grey Street) but he commissioned John and Benjamin Green to build an even more beautiful Theatre Royal in 1837 at the top of Upper Dene Street to replace it. Whilst a pupil of Stephenson, Dobson also became a student of painting under Boniface Moss, an Italian refugee with a studio in Newcastle and had John Martin of Haydon Bridge as a fellow pupil. Dobson wanted to improve his technique in drawing and painting (which was to be of great help to him in his career as a frequent exhibitor of watercolours of architectural subjects at the Royal Academy) and in 1810, after eight years with Stephenson, he resolved to go to London to deepen his knowledge of art in general. No-one preached more eloquently than Dobson the doctrine that architecture was only one branch of the visual arts, and that if an architect did not appreciate and understand other branches of art, his work as an architect would suffer. Dobson never travelled further abroad than France and never visited either Greece or Italy (and doubtless as a classicist felt the same inferiority for this omission that Dr. Johnson felt); but he compensated for this by an intensive study of the drawings and paintings of the classical world—especially architectural drawings. He would have sympathised with the cultural philosophy underlying Frank West Rich's remark in his address to his fellow architects[8]—"Be a gentleman first and an architect afterwards".

When Dobson and Rich stressed the importance of all the Arts to

Architecture, they were returning to the conception of the Architect as Supreme Artist. This concept was the very essence of Palladianism, and when in 1606 Inigo Jones' friend Edmund Bolton presented him with a book inscribed —"To his own Inigo Jones through whom there is hope that sculpture, modelling, architecture, painting, acting and all that is praiseworthy in the eloquent arts of the Ancients may one day find their way across the Alps into our England".[9] When in addition to this Inigo Jones was the designer of costume and scenery for the Royal Masque, an antiquarian, a man of affairs with a seat in the House of Commons, one can see that Bolton's faith had much to support it; and when Dobson designed furniture for Beaufront Castle, and for the dining room and bedrooms of Lilburn Tower, as well as designing fireplaces, plaster-work, and the gilt wood pelmets in all his houses, and exhibited water-colours at the Royal Academy, and produced hundreds of topographical drawings on sketching tours with Sydney Smirke, one can see the working out of the old tradition.

So Dobson went to London and sought out John Varley. Varley was too busy and too successful to want a pupil, and refused him saying that if he gave him lessons it would have to be at five in the morning. This offer—meant to deter—Dobson immediately accepted. Dobson's eagerness so impressed Varley that he not only gave him lessons but invited him to stay in his home until Dobson could find lodgings, and they became life-long friends. One of Varley's watercolours exhibited at the Royal Academy testified to their friendship. It is called 'Dobson's dream', and was composed by Varley from a rough pencil sketch made by Dobson immediately on waking.

During this year in London Dobson formed lasting friendship with several distinguished men who seemed to recognise his quality—Turner, Mulready and Benjamin West amongst them. He also met the Smirke family and moved in their circle. Robert[10] (later to be Sir Robert) was then twenty-nine years of age and was to be made R.A. the next year (1811). He was already a Grecian devotee and it has been suggested that it was due to his influence rather than to Monck's that Dobson developed such an early sympathy for the Classical. The influence of both these distinguished men on the young Dobson must have been considerable. He also met Robert's younger brother, Sydney, then twelve years of age, who was later to rebuild Robert's Carlton Club, to design the domed reading room of the British Museum and the new home of the Royal

Academy at Burlington House, and was to become Dobson's son-in-law by marrying his eldest daughter.[11]

In 1811, against the advice of his new friends, who urged him to set up practice in London, he returned to Newcastle to find at first as he said "that it was easier to profess an art than to practise it". But after his meeting with Monck in about 1811 or 1812, and after his work at Belsay, the commissions began to flow and were never to diminish during the next fifty one years.

In spite of what both Dobson and his daughter, Margaret Jane, say about his early difficulties and his slow start in practice, what strikes an observer is his extremely quick progress. By 1813 he was making large additions to Gibside House for Lord Strathmore, transforming Chees-burn for the Riddell family, making alterations to James Paine's Bradley Hall for Lord Ravensworth, and was engaged on the designing of his first Church—the Scotch Church at North Shields. By 1815 he was making additions to Falloden for the Grey family, and was not only restoring Vanbrugh's Seaton Delaval, but adding a new wing there for Sir Jacob Astley. This retiring and modest young man must have possessed much quiet charm to be entrusted so quickly with such important work for the leading families in the North.

But it is the elegance of Prestwick Lodge (1815) which most clearly illustrates what were to be characteristic Dobson features. It is a little gem of a three-bay villa (page 31), a miniature Mitford Hall (page 44) with ornate iron staircase balusters, and chimneypieces and pelmet rails also designed by Dobson (similar to those at Nunnykirk). A large stair-head window makes sure that none of the fine detail is missed. The front portico is Doric, and the pillars in the hallway are also fluted Doric. It is a Greek temple but on the smallest possible domestic scale.

Prestwick showed also another Dobson characteristic—the beauti-fully cut and finely jointed blocks of sandstone which make the house. In Dobson's houses the mortar between the large and beautifully cut stone is so fine that you can scarcely see it. They look like dry stone houses, so perfect is the mason's work. The standard of masonry is such that Dobson must have employed for many years the same teams of local masons—and their work is not excelled anywhere.

One of the most important qualities of Dobson is the trouble he took to enter into and discover what he called "the true spirit of the place", when considering the design and siting of his buildings. His sensitivity as

Yarmouth Church, initialled and dated 1839. (*Laing Art Gallery*)
This and the three following illustrations are from a Dobson Sketch Book

Hampton Court. (*Laing Art Gallery*)

14

Gainsborough Old Hall (East front) initialled and dated 1831. (*Laing Art Gallery*)

Gainsborough Old Hall (North front) initialled and dated 1831. (*Laing Art Gallery*)

an artist ensured that the relationship between building and landscape was correct. On visiting a Dobson house one feels the siting of it is the only possible one, but there is a particular subtlety in the choice of direction in which the house faces which must be mentioned. His houses, great or small, rarely had the front entrance facing the view. As Dobson said in his Presidential address[12] of 1859 to the Northern Architectural Association— 'Our friends from the south find too often occasion to complain of the cold blasts with which we are apt to receive them. I have designed many mansions of various sizes in different parts of England, and one of my first objects has been so to plan the house that I might have the entrance where it is least commanding in its view; this affords me an opportunity of planting out the entrance front, so that the strong winds are checked as much as possible'. This technique is particularly notice-able and successful at Beaufront Castle and at Mitford, both houses built on elevated sites where the winds blow across great expanses of landscape against windows showing a fine view but which need not be opened, whilst at the other side of the house away from the view the entrance front is protected by Dobson's shrubberies and plantations.
Of Sir John Vanbrugh, Dobson said,

> His style was founded on the Italian, but in his efforts to produce a striking effect by picturesque outline and breadth of light and shade, he cared little about the minor elegances of Italian art, and indeed degenerated sometimes into grotesqueness. His interiors were grand and full of display, to suit the gay and voluptuous manners of the times—but they were accomplished at the sacrifice of convenience and comfort—Sir John's general plan was to enter the building direct from the north into a magnificent hall, with corridors leading right and left; the consequence was that the current of air from the exterior was unchecked and rendered the building in cold weather almost uninhabitable. The late Lord Strathmore who was a constant visitor at Seaton Delaval complained to me of the want of comfort and that he felt obliged always to have an extra cloak with him when residing there. When the property became Sir Jacob Astley's, I was engaged to restore the house but I do not remember ever feeling comfortable in any of the apartments, not even at the dinner table. The capacious and hospitable fireplace of Sir Jacob's dining room served but to quicken the currents of cold air that found their way through the ample avenues of that noble but comfortless abode.

Dobson's practice grew fast. He rose at 5 a.m. and worked until after midnight and continued to do this until his stroke two years before his death. His attention to detail was meticulous, and even in these early years the variety and amount of work astonishes. In addition to the many commissions for houses, churches, public buildings, warehouses, hospitals, bridges, he designed in 1818 the artificial lake and landscape at Bolam, in 1822 the Gothic and castellated Morpeth gaol (now the Morpeth courthouse), in 1823 Angerton Hall near Morpeth, an exercise in Tudor and Gothic. in the same year he completed the classical transformation of Trollop's Guildhall begun by Stephenson and Newton in 1796, and at its East end covered in the old open columned fish market. In 1824 he was commissioned by Richard Grainger to begin his designs for the new Eldon Square. This was the first intimation on any grand scale of the coming transformation of Newcastle by Grainger into the only town in England with a neo-classical commercial centre.

As to Eldon Square (now demolished and the site made unlovely by a vast shopping precinct) Pevsner wrote:[13]

> . . . here indeed a claim to formality and monumentality was staked that was new to the town and must at once have doomed the modest houses of Saville Row. It must of course not be forgotten that at that time nothing yet existed of Grainger Street and Grey Street, that is the centre of Newcastle, and except for Mosley Street[14] was still narrow and unplanned. The spaciousness of Eldon Square was a thing quite unheard-of. So was the size of the ranges surrounding the square, and so was also their uniform design. The three ranges of houses are treated each as one individual block. They are connected only by walls; the blocks have two-and-a-half storeys and look into the square from each floor with twenty-seven windows on East and West and thirty-nine on the North. Each range is composed in the accepted Palladian fashion of, e.g. John Nash's recent terraces around Regent's Park, that is with accents on the angles and the centre. The accents consist of giant Doric pilasters. In addition the five-bay centre on the North side had enlarged floor heights and a bigger attic. Along the first floor run pretty cast iron balconies with Grecian honeysuckle decorations. No more is done to show the superior quality of these houses. It was however enough to set a new standard characterised by the use of ashlar, worked with great precision and in contrast to Nash's and the Regent's taste in London an almost complete abstention from ornament.

This book is not about Grainger and his transformation of Newcastle;[15] nor is it about the buildings Dobson planned to build and did not. But it should be said that Grainger showed little or no interest in any grandiose re-planning of Newcastle's town centre until about 1831; and before that date the only plans put forward to the Corporation had been by Dobson in 1824 and by his fellow architect, Thomas Oliver, the designer of the vast and impressive Leazes Terrace. Dobson's plan of grand and dignified squares linked by immensely wide tree-lined streets anticipated as a necessity and recommended the purchase of Major Anderson's property (Anderson Place) consisting of 13 acres in the centre of Newcastle. Dobson proposed to build on Anderson Place (amongst other things) a Mansion House described by McKenzie[16] as a 'civic palace . . . to have four handsome stone fronts, the North, South and West sides to rise from a bold terrace and the latter front to be ornamented with eight beautiful pillars. The East front to face Pilgrim Street to have a lofty grand portico, capable of admitting carriages . . .'

Dobson's plan was well received and would in fact have given Newcastle a centre even more elegant than Grainger's. McKenzie wrote,[17] "Mr. Dobson, architect, has offered plans for the appropriation of this ground (Anderson Place) which seems in the highest degree to combine elegance with utility". Dobson's plan was however hugely expensive, he lacked financial backing, and as his daughter regretfully wrote in her Memoir, "he had the fastidiousness of a retiring nature", and it was the ebullient and bold Grainger who in 1834 won Town Clerk Clayton's official and financial backing for his plans.

1834, the year when Grainger got the backing of the Corporation for his redevelopment plan and bought the 13 acres of Anderson Place (as Dobson had proposed) for £50,000, is the most important year in Newcastle's architectural history. Before 1834, the Woods had built graceful crescents in Bath, and Adam had built squares and terraces in Edinburgh—but they were almost entirely residential development. The uniqueness of Grainger's plan lay in the fact that he intended to build, not houses alone in the city centre, but whole streets of gracious shops and public buildings and shopping arcades, with living quarters for the shopkeepers above them; and all were to be built in the beautiful Kenton stone in the Neo-classical style with, above the shop fronts, ornate pillars and capitals, pilasters, pediments and friezes based on Greek designs. It was not only a unique achievement in 1834 but in scale and beauty it has never been equalled in this country since—and certainly not by the stucco of Nash's Regent Street.

But Grainger was a builder of genius, not an architect, even although in the confusion of his time as to the distinction he is often called one, and indeed was so called in his obituary. But whilst Grainger knew the character and scale of what he wanted, and doubtless told his designers, Wardle, Walker, Oliver, John and Benjamin Green, and Dobson, what he wanted, he was not the sort of man to go to the expense of keeping a dog and attempting to bark himself. There is no known evidence that Grainger ever designed anything himself, but his influence was overpowering, and a designer would get his drawings back for amendment if they did not please him. Grainger was fortunate in that in 1834 Newcastle happened to have in practice a group of the most talented designer-builders and architects in the town's history, all well versed in classical architecture thanks to the tradition and example of Stephenson and Stokoe—and in Northumberland of Monck and Paine. The architects in their turn were fortunate to be working for a developer who wanted to enrich his town with the best, and who had an appreciation of fine decoration, and who spoke nothing but the truth when he told the Cholera Commissioners of 1854 that, "he had a taste for art and was not bound to decorate his houses in the manner the Commissioners had seen, but did it because it pleased him to do it, though the cost had probably been not less than £100,000". Wardle and Walker were designers who were then employed by Grainger in 1834 in his office. All the others mentioned above were in practice in Newcastle on their own account.

After Eldon Square (1824), one of Dobson's most important contributions to Grainger's massive transformation of the town was the porticoed and beautiful[18] Royal Arcade, a shopping and office Arcade that formed a noble conclusion looking along Mosley Street, standing like a Parthenon on top of the rise towards Pilgrim Street, The Royal Arcade was completed in May 1832 and took eleven months to build. It cost Grainger £40,000 and is undoubtedly one of the most beautiful buildings Dobson ever designed. At its entrance were two massive Doric pillars (see page 79) and its interior consisted of an avenue of pilasters and columns 250 ft long, 20 ft. wide, and 35 ft. high. The floor consisted of squares of block marble. On each side of the avenue were eight large shops and over the shops were the first floor offices occupied by solicitors, architects and engineers.

Dobson's roofs repay close study. Of all the remarkable Dobson roofs that are illustrated in this book, from the domed roofs and glass centrepieces of his country houses to the curving iron roof of his Central Railway Station and the timbered roofing of the vegetable market, the glass domed roof of the Royal Arcade is perhaps the most beautiful of all.

The roof arches spring from the top of the great pilasters of the avenue to support the domes, and both the arches and the dome interiors are heavily decorated with ironwork tracery (see page 90). A Newcastle newspaper proclaimed, 'We do not believe that as an Arcade, this of Newcastle has its equal in Europe or in the Universe'. It was not Dobson's fault that it was sited too near the river and too far away from Grainger's new streets to be a commercial success.

Dobson also designed (1834) the East side of Grey Street, that is the plainer side, whilst on the ornate side Wardle may have designed the Bank of England (surely one of the most beautiful bank buildings in England) which was originally two houses built by Grainger. Wardle and Walker designed Grainger and Clayton Streets.

In 1828 Dobson had designed No. 41 Blackett Street[19] with beautiful attached columns *in antis*. It was the headquarters of T. M. Richardson's Northern Academy of Art, the artistic centre of the town, a stone oasis in the drab brick of Oliver's Blackett Street. Dobson also designed the new markets—the vegetable market with its fine timbered roof (now covered by the Corporation) and the butcher market with its pilastered arcades, 360 windows, fanlights and wood cornices, and four avenues each 338 feet long. These markets, the largest in the provinces, were the most successful attempts at a shopping precinct Newcastle has ever achieved and not only because, owing to the low rents and overheads they could (and still do) sell goods cheaper than shops in the main streets. The markets were opened on the 24th October 1835. To celebrate their opening a great dinner was held in the Vegetable Market, attended by 2,000 guests and presided over by the Mayor.[20] The speeches are preserved and it does not seem that there was any mention of the architect, Dobson. It is not easy to realise today, with the fine roofs boarded over and the modern modifications of the original designs, that these markets are (or were) of great architectural elegance, as a study of the photographs on pages 91 and 93 will make plain. They cover several acres in extent, and the interior consists of five longitudinal avenues and four transverse ones each twelve feet wide and 'present a succession of arched passages between the longer avenue'. The Butcher Market at its opening had 188 shops.

The Vegetable Market has an avenue of 338 feet long, 57 feet wide, 40 feet high and contained 55 shops when it was opened. On page 93 the metal pillars can be seen carrying longitudinal beams supporting the magnificent timbered roof. A contemporary work[21] described the roof as follows:

> Two ranges of strong quadrangular metal pillars, 45 in each range, divide the area into a centre and side aisle, and support longitudinal beams on which is reared the firm and beautiful framework of the roof. That of the side aisles is supported by open spandrels fixed in the walls, on which are laid horizontal beams reaching to the longitudinal ones just mentioned, and adorned in the middle of each with a massive corbel. Above the longitudinal beams, a higher range, supported by uprights and stretchers, are connected across the centre of the area by transverse beams, which are supported to about one fourth of their length from each side by curved spandrels. From these points upright posts, the lower extremity of each being decorated with a corbel, support the sloping rafters of the upper part of the roof. Each side of the highest compartment or clerestory forms one entire window from end to end; and the Market is further lighted and ventilated by 42 windows with swing sashes in each of the side walls. In a recess at one end of the Market is a clock. In the centre, and opposite the intersection of the second and third transverse avenues are two massive and elegantly shaped stone fountains, the basin of each capable of containing 3,000 gallons. (see the photographs).

In Dobson's day such pleasure and pride was taken in the Markets by the town that they were used for tea parties and as Collard and Ross put it, 'for the immense annual assemblages of children belonging to the Sunday schools of the town and neighbourhood'. In 1838 the Market was used as an assembly and promenade for the town's distinguished guests during the visit of The British Association to Newcastle. In addition to the ornate gas lamps attached to the pillars, there were 'flags, variegated lamps and festoons of flowers and evergreens . . .; and wreaths of gas lights, placed around the shafts of the fountains, sparkled through the trickling water which fell around them like the preternatural illumination of a fairy palace'.[22]

Dobson is too good an architect with too many beautiful buildings to his credit (although much of his Newcastle work is either under threat or has been demolished) to need the attribution to him of works he did not do. Perhaps it is the result of Dobson's daughter's 1885 *Memoir* in which everthing good is claimed for Dobson (even Oliver's Leazes Terrace), and in which she plainly thinks that too much credit has been accorded to Grainger because all the designs, she says, were her father's. Most writers have tended to follow her wholesale attribution to Dobson of the new developments, Pevsner declaring[23] 'Grey Street is no doubt the best of Dobson's city streets and one of the best streets in England . . . Dobson himself clearly regarded Grey Street as the climax of his Newcastle work', whilst Richard Welford in 1895, a Newcastle man himself, wrote[24] – 'to Mr. Dobson's fine perceptions of the true and beautiful, Newcastle owes the fine line of streets which were erected by Richard Grainger'.

The truth of the matter is that the further one gets away in time from 1834-36, when most of the new streets were built, the more it is accepted that apart from the Greens' designing of the Theatre Royal and the Earl Grey statue, all the street designs are by Dobson, and men like Wardle and Walker disappear completely from architectural history for well over 100 years. The nearer, however, one approaches the time when the new streets were built, the more one hears of designers other than Dobson being responsible, although there is no doubt that Dobson was frequently consulted by Grainger and advised him. For example, on 3rd June 1837 this editorial comment on Grey Street appeared in the Newcastle Journal.

> . . . the buildings just adverted to will complete the west side of Grey Street, the centre three ranges of which as well as the western half of Market Street and Grainger Street, it is but justice to say have been entirely designed in Mr. Grainger's office by Mr. Wardle under Mr. Grainger's immediate direction.

The Editorial also stated that Wardle designed the south side of Shakespeare Street, the north side of which was the work of John and Benjamin Green as part of their design for the Theatre Royal. Since all the designers were alive and well when this Editorial appeared and since it called forth no protests or denials, it seems that the editorial must have been accurate, all the more so since on 21st March 1869 a singularly well informed letter appeared in the Newcastle Daily Chronicle confirming the statements in the editorial of 3rd June 1837 and declaring;

> The Butcher and Green Markets—were designed by the late Mr. John Dobson, who also designed that portion of the East side of Grey Street which reaches from Shakespeare Street to Mosley Street . . . all the rest of the new streets, including part of Grey Street, Grainger Street, Market Street, Clayton Street, etc. etc. were designed by the late Mr. John Wardle. The Central Exchange was not Mr. Dobson's design but Mr. Wardle's assisted by Mr. George Walker.

It is important to bear in mind that Dobson's contribution to the Grainger transformation of Newcastle, great though it was, took up only a relatively small part of his time, and that the work was done side-by-side with his other commissions including those of his first love—the designing of country houses, and it is of these country houses that something more should now be said.

CHAPTER TWO

THE DOBSON COUNTRY HOUSE

A seventeenth or eighteenth Century country house, with the plaster-work, chimneypieces and doorcasings of its period, its collection of paintings and porcelain, its books and furniture, is not only acknowledged to be England's most singular contribution to the decorative arts, but must seem to many to be the nearest thing to felicity that human beings have yet achieved. Even on a more modest scale, a surviving terrace of houses with fanlights of delicate tracery and ornate iron balconies above, both delight and make us sad at what has gone from our world. Viewed with the knowledge of what was to come, Dobson's classical country houses, built between 1815 and 1832, can be seen as the final flowering of Georgian craftsmanship and design before they—and much else—disappeared.

Perhaps Dobson was fortunate in that the North lagged many years behind fashionable London taste, and it was still possible to go on building decent plain houses of Georgian proportion until the 1840s, and Northumberland was saved by its backwardness from many of the fevered Victorian transcriptions of Renaissance Palace and the medieval Castle which are (or were), so frequently to be found in the more fashionable and wealthy counties nearer London.

It has already been mentioned that Prestwick Lodge (1815) is not only the earliest classical Dobson house (and one of his most successful), but that he also designed the iron staircase balustrades, the pelmet rods, and the main chimneypieces. In this meticulous designing of the detail (which extended to cornices, plasterwork, bookcases and sometimes to the furniture) Dobson was following the example set by Adam, Kent and others. At Lilburn Tower[25] (page 48) he designed the dining room furniture and the bookcases made by Thomas Wallace and Sons, a Newcastle firm of joiners, and there is furniture made to Dobson's design at Beaufront, also by the same firm. Just as the unsurpassed quality of the stonework of his houses points to Dobson using the same team of masons again and again, so he used the local craftsmen who had helped him in previous commissions—Waterson,[26] the stonemason who carved Dobson's design for the drawing room chimneypiece at Beaufront (page 64), Cuthbert Burnhope the joiner who carved Dobson's wooden chimneypiece in this same house (page 60) and the plasterer, Ralph Dodds, whose name is commemorated in the foundations both of Lilburn (1828) and Beaufront (1835-41).

At Beaufront there is still William Cuthbert's account book showing the names of the workmen concerned in the building of the house, the work they did and the amounts they received. The only two amounts shown for Dobson's fees as architect total a modest £250, far less than some craftsmen received.

Dobson plainly treated the craftsmen with respect. When the foundation stone of Lilburn Tower was laid on 3rd January 1829[27] there was buried in the foundations a manuscript commemorating not only the names of Thomas Wallace and Sons, the Newcastle joiners and the Ralph Dodds already mentioned, but Robert Wallace, clerk of works, and Robert Hall the mason from Alnwick.

Of the classical houses, Mitford Hall (pages 44, 45) is a larger version of Prestwick and was built in 1828, although the plans had existed from 1823. The siting of the house is superb, the drawing room windows looking down to the river Wansbeck, to Mitford Church and to the massive castle mound, crowned by the ruins of the Mitford's first home—Mitford Castle. Still to be seen from the windows is the tall entrance tower, the sole remains with the kitchen, of the Mitford's second home—Mitford Manor House.[28] The Mitfords (*men of the midford*) have owned land in the area since early in the 11th Century at least, and Dobson clearly saw the importance of their third home preserving the visual link with their two previous ones.

Hodgson's *History of Northumberland* (Part 2, Vol. II) published in 1832 states –

The new Manor House, the shell of which is in progress in 1828 is a very handsome square edifice built from designs by Mr. Dobson. The beautiful white sandstone of which its outside walls are built is obtained from a stratum of rock which forms the bed of the Font. Great praises is due to the owner for choosing a stone for his new residence which is not only beautiful but has every appearance of being indestuctible to atmospheric agents. The site of the house is well chosen. This is a fertile and most delightful place.

Mitford shows the deep decorative cornices (pages 8, 44) the iron balustrades, the Doric portico, the Dobson-designed chimneypieces and the large windows which let the countryside flow into the house. Mitford and Meldon Park (1832) have almost the identical type of conservatories with alternating pilasters and windows and both have the same Italianate stable clock towers.

Dr Girouard has shown[29] that Dobson's plans for his early large houses are very similar to John Shaw's plan for Cresswell House on the Northumberland coast which was begun in 1821 just before Dobson began Doxford Hall (1822). John Shaw was a London architect and Cresswell House was unfortunately demolished in the 1930s. Because Shaw's plan preceded any of Dobson's largest houses one may conclude that he was influenced by Shaw's lay-out, but the standard of workmanship, the design and decorative aspects of Dobson's work which so impresses to-day is not derived from Shaw. Dr Girouard sums up the design as follows-

> In the main block of the house, the principal living rooms are grouped like an L along two facades, with a bold bay window on the facade nearest the entrance front. Within the smaller L is a square containing a study, or some such room, and these three interlocking elements—main living rooms, hall with staircase, and study, make up the main block of the house. To one side of this is a long service wing, and at right angles to the service wing is a conservatory.

Dobson's smaller houses do not confirm to this plan nor does Nunnykirk in which Dobson had the difficult problem of integrating into his design an older existing house, and solved it brilliantly. But of course it is not the plan which strikes the visitor, to Longhirst for example, but the magnificently veined and worked sandstone, the pillared entrance portico, the elegant staircase with the iron work decorated with honeysuckle and other Greek motifs, dividing to form separate stairways up to an upper gallery extending round the whole upper floor, the upper gallery rail having the same classical motif as the stairway; and above this gallery is the domed roof of the open hall with its glass centrepiece (see page 47).

At Longhirst the pillars of the portico are Corinthian and go almost up to the roof of the house. It is the most melodramatic front of all Dobson's houses. At Meldon Park and Nunnykirk the entrance porticos are Ionic, at Mitford Doric. Longhirst is further remarkable in that the oval hall, the stairs, galleries, and walls above the hallway are of naked sandstone, making the interior even more powerful (*cf*. Vanburgh) than the other Dobson domed halls such as Nunnykirk which have plaster ceilings and walls. Some of the stone blocks at Longhirst and Meldon are enormous weighing up to eight tons. At Longhirst the ceiling above the hallway with its glass centerpiece is triple-domed.

At Nunnykirk Dobson visually married the old house of the Ord family into the new by the strong external horizontal rustication. This old house is clearly seen in the high centre of the south front, (page 42), and Dobson largely repeated his Longhirst design for the domed hall, reiterating Shaw's feature of the bold bow-window near to the entrance front, (see page 42) enclosing a small bow-ended drawing room. This drawing room, when last I visited it, also had convoluting and elaborate gilt-wood pelmets similar to those at Prestwick, and the original paper was still on its walls. At Meldon Park in the 1920's Lutyens substituted the present wooden balusters on the stairway for Dobson's iron work (page 58).

Nothing was allowed to interfere with the purity of Dobson's country house. All drainpipes and plumbing were installed and run down internally, so that no sign of them shows on the face of the building itself, a remarkable anticipation of modern practice, and not without dangers.

As to the Tudor-Gothic designs exemplified by such houses as Beaufront and Lilburn Tower, the core of the house still remained classical despite the turrets, towers, and square mullioned windows. The arrangement of the rooms is the same as at Meldon Park and Longhirst, the same unusually large window on the half landing illuminating the detail,[30] the same high hallway and ironwork balustrading except that here the detail has a Gothic flavour and instead of the classical portico there is a large castellated porte-cochère. The verdict of one architectural historian[31] is that 'Dobson's dexterity in translating Greek into Tudor must be admired for the result is completely successful'. The extra cost involved in departing from the straight lines and simplicity of the classical design into the realm of the picturesque, is shown by the fact that the cost of Meldon Park (1832) was £7,188-1s-11d, excluding the stables, whilst the cost of the turrets and towers of Lilburn (1828) was £21,975, (also excluding the stables) Beaufront cost more than £30,000.

In Dobson's Tudor-Gothic houses there is little sign of the heavy semi-ecclesiastical portentousness which is so often characteristic of such houses. Dobson's houses retain something of the classical lightness of touch as the drawing room at Lilburn (page 54) and as the stable courtyard at Beaufront (page 61) show. What is not lighthearted is strong, monumental and reminds one of the theatricality of Vanbrugh rather than the religiosity of Pugin. Adam's rococo Gothic at Alnwick Castle and the delightful work at Fowberry Tower in a similar style was probably known to John Dobson.

In both Lilburn and Beaufront the original designs of the fronts have been modified, at Beaufront by A. J. Hanson's addition of the low three-windowed smoking room, immediately adjacent to the entrance, (now demolished), and at Lilburn by moving the porte-cochère from midway between the two projecting wings to a position further to the right. This was done by Dobson himself at some time between 1840 and 1850, for reasons which are difficult to justify aesthetically, but which resulted in the front entrance not giving direct entry into the main hall but into a small side hall closed off from the main one, thereby preventing draughts from outside running straight through the main part of the building.

Lilburn Tower is particularly important for three reasons. First, because the parts of the house built by Dobson are almost without any subsequent alteration and are as Dobson built them; secondly because the house still contains so many pieces of furniture designed by Dobson for the house, and thirdly because of the spectacular beauty of the ceilings. The ballroom and drawing room ceilings are illustrated in this book (pages 48, 50).

The Dobson-designed furniture is as ingenious as it is striking. A sideboard in the dining room looks like a solid piece of furniture with no apparent doors or drawers of any kind, but it slides apart to reveal cupboards and drawers for wine, cutlery and linen. In the same bedroom as the wardrobe and the four poster bed is a bed-side table (page 00) that converts into a night commode. Here we have a glimpse of the ingenious architect who also designed machinery for rolling the curved iron principals of the roof in the Newcastle railway station.

The number of houses which Dobson re-modelled and transformed was even greater than the number of new houses he built. In this work he displayed a resourcefulness and sensitivity which won him a reputation reflected in the amount of work he was called upon to do all over the country. Cheesburn Grange is a good example of his remodelling work, and the plans he drew up in 1813 are works of art in themselves (see pages 36 to 38).

How simple Cheesburn was in the 18th Century can be seen from the painting in the possession of Mr Phillip Riddell which is dated 1791. The front entrance to the house was, in 1813, on the South elevation as shown on Dobson's drawing (page 34). Dobson moved the front entrance to the West front but preserved the beautiful 18th Century pillared stone doorway which he positioned in the garden where it still is. Having moved the entrance to the West, Dobson added the tower over the front door and built the chapel to the left of the entrance doorway. The modern photograph shows that the present West elevation of the house is still almost exactly as Dobson remodelled it, because although the corner turrets are drawn on Dobson's plan, they were never built. The South elevation too is shown on Dobson's plan, before and after he had remodelled it and taken the entrance doorway away, and is much the same to-day. The green-and-gold drawing room is a gracious characteristically Dobson room with gilt-wood pelmet rods that are extremely fine, and the room shows little sign of A. J. Hanson's 1860 work.

The watercolour drawings of the lodge and entrance gates, taken from the 1813 plan, which are enlarged and reproduced here (page 41) are so decorative as to make one regret all the more that so few of Dobson's original plans and drawings have survived.

Dobson's houses were not built for the great and noble landed families whose houses, executed by Vanbrugh, Adam, Kent or Paine were built to a scale that created melodramatic palaces in a landscape. Dobson's houses were built for the county gentry, or for manufacturers or professional men who wished to become gentry. It must seem to many that their appeal is enhanced by their domestic scale. The classical houses in particular seem masterpieces in their own right and Sir Nikolaus Pevsner has called them 'noble designs which established him at once as one of the best amongst the architects of his generation in England'.[32]

Prestwick Lodge, 1815, the Hall and Stair
*(By permission of Mrs I. S. Duncan. Photograph by Ken Hitcham,
Philipson Studios)*

The Dining room, Prestwick Lodge (*K. Hitcham, Philipson Studios*)
'In Prestwick, Dobson's earliest large house, the detail is firmly rooted in the
18th Century'

Giltwood pelmet rod from Prestwick. (*Ken Hitcham, Philipson Studios*)

Prestwick Lodge, Sitting room ceiling
(*Ken Hitcham, Philipson Studios*)

33

South Elevation of the HOUSE in it's present ftate.

CHEESBURN GRANGE, South Elevation before Dobson's remodelling, 1813, Drawing by Dobson
(By courtesy of Major Philip Riddell as are the drawings which follow)

Cheesburn Grange, from an eighteenth century painting

SOUTH ELEVATION

Cheesburn Grange, South Elevation showing Dobson's proposed remodelling with turrets

WEST ELEVATION

Cheesburn Grange, West Elevation as proposed by Dobson

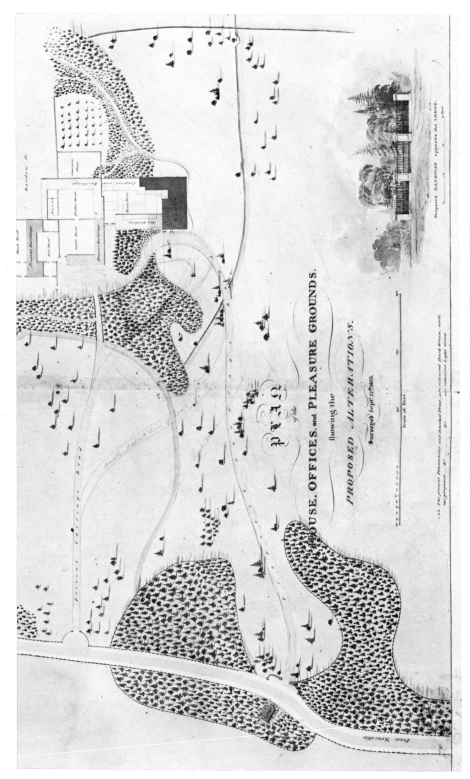

Dobson's plan for Cheesburn Grange, 1813

Cheesburn Grange, South Elevation as it was built and is today. The turrets
were never built and the parapet was added by A. J. Hanson in 1870.
West Elevation today with Dobson's chapel on the left of the front entrance.
(Ken Hitcham, Philipson Studios)

Proposed GATEWAY opposite the LODGE.

Dobson's drawing for gates at Cheesburn Grange (not executed).

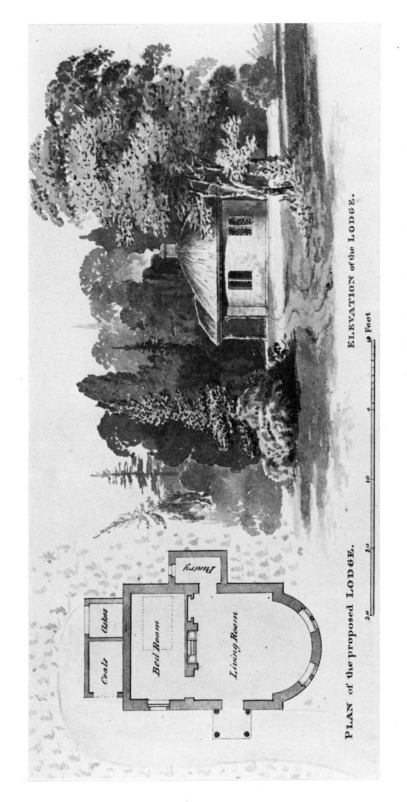

PLAN of the proposed LODGE.

Luery

Ashes

Coals

Bed Room

Living Room

ELEVATION of the LODGE.

10 Feet

Dobson's plan and watercolour of a lodge for Cheesburn Grange (not executed).

NUNNYKIRK 1825. Above: the front entrance with Ionic pillared porch.
Below: the garden front. Dobson integrated the old house seen in the centre
into the remodelling by means of heavy horizontal rustication.
(Photographs, Country Life)

Nunnykirk, the Hall *(Country Life)*

43

MITFORD HALL; (designed 1823, built 1828). Entrance front and Doric portico.
Dobson designed chimneypiece and cornice in the drawing room.
(By courtesy of Brigadier and Mrs Mitford. Photographs, Ken Hitcham, Philipson Studios)

Mitford Hall showing staircase, balusters and landing ceiling.
(*Ken Hitcham, Philipson Studios*)

LONGHIRST HALL, 1828, The 'Corinthian' Portico. *(Country Life)*
The columns are a modification of Greek Corinthian with volutes derived from
the Roman Composite order. The cornice is nearer to Doric. Dobson used the
Greek style with taste and considerable freedom.

Longhirst Hall, the upper gallery and domed ceiling with glass centrepiece.
The hall and stairway: all walls are of dressed sandstone. *(Country Life)*

LILBURN TOWER, 1828, The Drawing Room. (*Country Life*)
'Although the motifs are Gothic, the Classical is never far away.'
(*By courtesy of Mr and Mrs Duncan Davidson*)

48

Lilburn Tower: Watercolour by John Dobson. (*Laing Art Gallery Collection*)

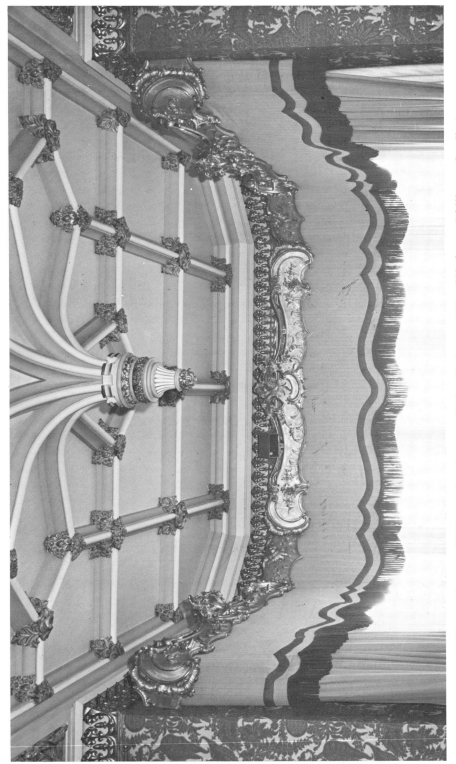

Lilburn Tower: "Giltwood pelmet rod" by Dobson. (*Ken Hitcham, Philipson Studios*)

Lilburn Tower: a bedroom with furniture designed by Dobson
*(By courtesy of Mr and Mrs Duncan Davidson. Photographs, Ken Hitcham,
Philipson Studios)*
51

Lilburn Tower: the dining room with furniture designed by Dobson
(Country Life)

52

Lilburn Tower: the staircase. Stairhead window by William Wailes and commissioned by Dobson. (*Country Life*)

Lilburn Tower: detail of drawing room ceiling.
(Ken Hitcham, Philipson Studios)

54

Lilburn Tower: the staircase

MELDON PARK, 1832, the Ionic Entrance Porch. *(Country Life)*

Meldon Park, watercolour by John Dobson. (*Laing Art Gallery Collection*)

Meldon Park: the hall and stairway. The wooden stair balustrade is by Sir
Edwin Lutyens and replaced in the 1920's Dobson's iron balusters. Lutyens
also added some Rococo plaster work which can be seen. *(Country Life)*
(By courtesy of Michael Cookson Esq.)

Meldon Park: The Garden Front. *(Country Life)*

Meldon Park: The Library. *(Country Life)*

BEAUFRONT CASTLE
Designed 1835 and completed in 1841
The West Front Entrance
(Country Life)

The triple-windowed single storey smoking room, by A. J. Hanson, adjoining the entrance has been demolished.

Beaufront Castle: The Stable Courtyard. *(Country Life)*
'A Monumentality reminiscent of Vanbrugh'

Beaufront Castle: The Staircase
Glass by William Wailes
(*Country Life*)

62

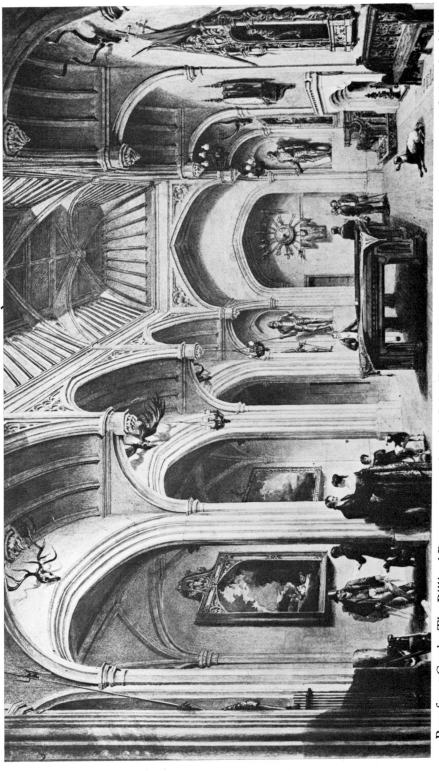

Beaufront Castle: The Billiard Room, watercolour by John Dobson. Dobson shows himself on extreme left showing his plans to William Cuthbert, the owner of the house. (*Country Life*)

Beaufront Castle: The Drawing Room with a Dobson chimney piece
(*Country Life*)

Beaufront Castle: Pelmet board and window casing
(By courtesy of Aidan Cuthbert Esq. Photograph, Ken Hitcham, Philipson Studios)

Jesmond Cemetery Lodge and gates, 1839
(Photograph, Ursula Clark)

The creation and landscaping of Bolam Lake in 1818 had been one of Dobson's earliest and most ambitious schemes of landscape gardening. But in 1839 Dobson not only designed Jesmond Cemetery Gates, its Church and its Dissenters' Chapel, but laid out the whole interior of the cemetery and planted it. There are of course no contemporary photographs of the layout (and the cemetery is now sadly in decay), but it is apparent from the comments at the time how much Dobson's scheme differed from the usual crowded and gloomy burial ground. His daughter wrote, "the cemetery is ornamentally laid out, and yet there is no mistaking it for a mere garden". *(See page 98).*

CHAPTER THREE

THE LATER WORK

Dobson's particular talent lay in adapting the Greek forms of architecture to the successful designing of houses large and small, to shops and streets, to schools—and even to railway stations. The Dobson-like railway station at Monkwearmouth (surely one of the most beautiful railway stations in Britain), is not however by Dobson, as generally believed, but is the work of Thomas Moore, a Sunderland architect who was one of the twenty seven original members who met in Newcastle on 13th November 1858 to form the Northern Architectural Association.

Dobson expressed in strong terms his view that railway stations as public buildings should not be built in the Gothic style, but in the simpler and more severe Classical style—and in spite of King's Cross, St. Pancras, and Sir John Betjeman, many would agree with him. In a lecture[33] Dobson said;

> Railway buildings ought to do much for architecture, being quite a new class of structures erected for purposes unknown until the present age—they suggest or ought to suggest a character of their own—; and being generally upon an extensive scale, they offer opportunities that have hitherto been of rare occurence. They are moreover especially public works—structures constantly seen by thousands and tens of thousands of persons, and might therefore do much towards improving the taste of the public —

Although Dobson's Newcastle Central Station with its portico, viewed today from Neville Street, is an extremely fine building, his original design, the watercolour of which was exhibited at the Royal Academy in 1850 and which won an award at the Paris Exhibition of 1858[34] is even more impressive. The building as it now is, and what Dobson wished it to be, can be compared (pages 81, 82), and it will be seen that Dobson's splendid double colonnaded front was rejected, as was the Italianate tower at the East end of the station. Even the portico was at first not accepted, but was eventually built (only partly in accordance with Dobson's second design) by Thomas Prosser, the Railway Company's own architect, in 1863 two years before Dobson's death and after he had retired to Ryton. The original design was described in *The Athenaeum* as, 'equal to Vanbrugh's grandest designs, and if executed will be the finest thing of its kind in Europe. Newcastle may be proud of its architect'.

However, even as it is, without the double colonnade and its tower, it must surely be considered (with Huddersfield and Monkwearmouth) one of the best of our railway stations[35]—especially when one considers the use of the curved iron ribs forming the principal arches of the curving station roof each 60 feet in width and following the curving line of the platforms. Dobson's daughter in her *Memoir*[36] says that this use of curved iron ribbing for roof support was then an architectural innovation—and it seems that in this she is correct, for Dobson himself in his 1859 address to his fellow architects (Apprendix One) claimed that with this use of curved iron he had originated an entirely new style of roofing.

This is important in any consideration of Dobson. The capacity to compose beautiful buildings is one thing, and a keen insight into the practical use of new methods and materials to solve old problems and serve new purposes is another—and the two qualities are rarely united in one man. Colvin states,[37] 'professionally he was unusually well equipped. From Varley he had acquired an enviable facility in producing enticing watercolour perspectives of his designs. To the skill of an artist he added the resourcefulness of an engineer and the practical competence of a surveyor'.

This practical or ingenious side of Dobson, in contrast to the aesthetic, emerges again and again. He pioneered a new method of eradicating dry rot, caused by dampness coming up from cellars and foundations, by placing a slight wall a few inches from the foundations, covering a vent on a level with the surface of the ground with perforated stones or flags so as to admit a thorough ventilation round the exterior of the building—this was considered at the time, says his daughter,[38] 'a real and important discovery'. When the lantern tower of St. Nicholas Church (not then a Cathedral), which Robert Stephenson calculated weighed 70 tons was in danger of collapse,[39] Dobson, in circumstances of difficulty and some danger, succeeded in widening the foundations of the 194 foot tower, supporting the walls by buttresses, taking down and restoring the pinnacles and all parts of the superstructure destroyed by age, and was particularly proud of the fact that nothing was to be seen externally of this restoration. When the foundations of Lambton Castle were subsiding owing to mining operations, Dobson filled the empty coal seams with continuous beds of masonry, carried down some of the principal walls of the castle fifteen feet below the cellars, and then underpinned those walls with a bed of concrete ten feet wide and to a further depth of eight feet. The magnitude of this operation was such that it took over six years to complete but the Castle was saved.

Until the 1850's the Georgian tradition was too near and too strong to allow Gothic that boldness and fantasy, which fed the 18th Century belief that it was a taste allied to madness. Churches built before the 1860's, although superficially Gothic, were often still essentially Georgian churches with Gothic additions. This is true even of Dobson's church St. Thomas the Martyr in Newcastle (1825). Although Dobson did here create a slim, soaring church whose pinnacles and towers reach high into the sky beyond its high arching ribbed roof, there is still, on the North side interior, a row of windows of precise Georgian proportion. We have seen that even in his Gothic houses at Beaufront and Lilburn, the classical is never very far away. We had to wait until there was a new generation of architects like Butterfield and, in Newcastle R. J. Johnson and T. R. Spence before churches could be built like St George's in Jesmond, Newcastle, (1888) by Spence with its striking Campanile, and St Matthew, Summerhill (1877) by Johnson.

But there is one church—the Clayton Memorial Church in Jesmond, Newcastle upon Tyne—designed by Dobson in 1858 and consecrated in 1861, which contradicts much that I have just written. Dedicated to the memory of Richard Clayton (brother of John Clayton who was until his death in 1856 Master of St Thomas' Church), its interior evokes—and how rare this is—the solemnity and the devotional atmosphere which most people can find only in much older churches. Yet it also looks forward to the simplicities that were to come thirty years later with the Arts and Crafts Movement, William Morris, Philip Webb and Dobson's successor in practice, R. J. Johnson. There is a complete absence of Victorian religiosity, only a stern strength relieved by symmetry, fine woodcarving and stained glass.

The East window glass which originally may have been a William Wailes design commissioned by Dobson, is no longer there having been destroyed in an air raid on 1st September 1941. The glass now in the East window is the work of Lawrence Lee who designed many of the windows for the new Coventry Cathedral. The stained glass in the West window was installed in 1906 and it must be said that both windows are at once rich, delicate, and refined, and far more successful than many of their period. The theme chosen for the West window was 'Lights of the Northumbrian Church' and depicts twelve famous North Country figures including Paulinus, King Edwin, King Oswald, St Aidan, St Wilfrid, St Cuthbert, the Venerable Bede and Bishop Ridley.

In this Dobson interior all irrelevant Gothic decoration is stripped away. It is a mid-19th Century church that looks to the past and to the future with astonishing perspicacity, and is one of the best churches of its period. The pattern of the roof timbers, black against a white background is oddly reminiscent (though built ten years before his birth!) of the Glasgow work of Charles Rennie Mackintosh. Prevsner's verdict is[40] 'a rarity after the ecclesiastical events of the Victorian age'.

The Clayton Memorial Church is one of Dobson's last churches. His earliest is the Scotch Church in Howard Street, North Shields, designed in 1811 and sited at the top of a stepped approach. It is a graceful Grecian building faced with Doric pilasters and is worthy of better treatment than it has received. It is now a Salvation Army Hall.

Dobson never built a classical church in Newcastle. However on page 84 is Dobson's own drawing[41] of a classical church dated 1840 which would have been St John, Elswick, had it ever been built. The plan states that the church is 'proposed to be built on a site presented by Richard Grainger in the centre of a line of dwelling houses which line is about to be built on the North side of Scotswood Road in the Parish of St Nicholas' and in the Parochial Chapelry of St John's'. Grainger's houses are seen on the left and right of the plan. The estimated cost was £3,361-0s-9d. It is a pity that 'The Commission for the Building of New Churches', set up to provide money to finance the building of new Anglican churches to match the explosion in the number of Non-Conformist chapels and churches in the industrial areas, withdrew support for the proposed church and deprived Newcastle of a most attractive building.

With the rarest exceptions, and in spite of their renewed interest in the Gothic, 19th Century architects laid too confident a hand on early church building, so that their 'restoration' of interiors destroyed much that was precious and often left them without character. John Green, the Newcastle architect, in 1840 dismantled the upper part of the Saxon tower of St. Batholomew's, Whittingham and substituted a higher and more impressive 'Gothic' top. Dobson himself was not immune from this insensitivity in church restoration and in the Norman church of St. Laurence, Warkworth he destroyed its clerestory, though his work in the Norman style at St. Andrews, Newcastle is more sensitive. Appreciation of the plain and crude early medieval work that our age finds so evocative was not often to be met with in Dobson's time. But the destruction of good architecture in Dobson's day was as nothing to what our own age has achieved since 1945, and at least the 19th Century kept the roof and exteriors in good repair and filled the church with worshippers.

I have not been able to trace any work done by Dobson for Grainger after 1841. By 1838 all the great Newcastle work was done, Grainger and Grey Streets, the Theatre Royal, and the many public buildings were completed. But in any event, the relationship between Grainger and Dobson had broken down by 1841.

Grainger owed Dobson a large sum of money for work done, and sought to reduce the sum by £250 by attempting to charge Dobson £250 for a 'staircase and painted ceiling taken from the mansion of the late Major Anderson and sent to Brinkburn Priory'. Dobson protested that it was Major Anderson who had originally bought the staircase and ceiling from Grainger, and that Dobson had merely acted as agent on behalf of the Major and that Grainger well knew this, that Major Anderson had then given the painted ceiling to his uncle, George Anderson, who had put it into store where it had been destroyed by fire, and that the staircase had in any event been badly damaged by Grainger's own workmen and was worth less than the £35 that its present owner, Major Cadogan of Brinkburn, had paid for it.

Dobson's reputation for good nature and honesty was and is beyond question, and his indignation is reflected in a letter[42] to the solicitor Percival Fenwick (for whom he had built Prestwick Lodge in 1815), writing that the only explanation for charging Dobson and involving Dobson in any way was 'to answer Mr. Grainger's present purpose'—*i.e.* to reduce the sum Grainger owed to Dobson—and continues, 'I really cannot imagine how Mr G. could have the impudence and want of feeling to have made such an attempt upon me—I have just seen Mr Joseph

Anderson who has promised to call on you to-morrow morning and let you have the agreement and will explain the facts above stated. I have also seen Mr George Anderson who will state to you the facts as regards the staircase—after such strange behaviour as this I cannot longer entertain that feeling of anxiety to serve a person in the manner I have striven and wished to do, that would treat me so shamefully if he could. I have therefore to request you will proceed without delay against him so that I may not be further imposed on by him'.

Dobson's indignation echoes down the years, and in a letter[42] dated April 2nd to Major Cadogon, owner of Brinkburn Priory in whose house, Brinkburn Grange, the staircase was to be installed, he wrote—

> Having a large sum due to me from Mr Grainger he has made a set-off charging me £250 for the painted ceiling and staircase taken from Anderson Place. I send you a copy of a letter written by me to Mr Percival Fenwick, solicitor, which will show you what a strange man Mr Grainger is—No doubt I shall bring him to act honestly in this transaction by preventing him being a rogue.

We now know what Dobson did not even suspect; that by April 1841 Grainger was in desperate financial trouble owing to his purchase in 1839 (with scarcely any money of his own) of John Hodgson Hinde's 800 acre Elswick Estate for £114,100. So serious was the outlook for Grainger that by 22nd September 1841 he was compelled to leave Newcastle for several weeks to avoid possible arrest for debt. It is sad that Grainger was reduced to the expedient described by Dobson for the paltry sum of £250. If Dobson had known of Grainger's plight he might have been less angry. So far as is known this brought about the final break-down of their professional relationship.

Dobson's work at Brinkburn had begun in 1830 and ended in 1837, so Grainger had waited for four years before attempting to charge Dobson for the staircase. In 1825 Major Cadogan had bought the Priory and a small stone house then on the site a few yards nearer to the river Coquet. Part of the older house with its two Georgian-Gothic windows on the river side and its rough stone work can still be seen to the East of Dobson's new West wing, (which now constitutes by far the greater part of the house), and is entered by a heavy Tudor style portico on the North side (away from the river) reminiscent of the work at Beaufront. On the South (the river side) two large Tudor mullioned windows dwarf the more delicate Georgian-Gothic arched windows of the original house.

Into the original East side of the house Dobson inserted the huge bow with the six Georgian-Gothic windows matching (except for their size) the two original windows on either side of Dobson's bow.

It must be said that this original East side with Dobson's great bow is the most successful and pleasing part of the house. The West wing with its tall chimneys, heavy portico and Tudor windows might have been more suited to a higher and more dominating site; but to build a large house and remodel an older house to become part of it, and to do this so close to the 12th Century Priory was a daunting task. The interior of Dobson's house (Brinkburn Grange) is now little more than a shell, but there is a delightful double-bow drawing room, a graceful staircase, and the remains of fine plasterwork on ceiling and cornice that proclaims the quality of the house. The Priory and house together constitute a site of outstanding architectural importance and is now in the care of the Department of the Environment.

In 1849 Dobson became involved as an expert witness in a legal action concerning the loss of timber profits by alleged neglect of the area he had landscaped around Bolam Hall in 1816-1818 for the Hon. Charles Beresford (later Lord Decies).

Dobson's[43] affidavit provides insight into his views and methods of landscape gardening.

> In 1816 I was employed by Lord Decies in laying out an artificial lake, the necessary Islands and adjoining Plantations at Bolam in the County of Northumberland. I have occasionally seen them in passing and observed that proper attention was not paid to thinning the trees so as to afford the necessary space for vigorous upper and undergrowth and to afford space for planting hollies and other evergreen underwood—to carry out the design intended by producing the required variety and extent of the lake by encouraging the healthy growth of the trees and underwood on the banks and Islands.
>
> I have not until yesterday seen the place for a few years—and I regret to say I found it in a neglected state owing entirely to the neglect of progressive thinning,—the trees are spindled up and without lateral branches and the underwood destroyed, thereby exposing the lake to view from the Public road—the same has taken place on the artificial Islands which ought to have been clothed with Brushwood topped with spruce and trees of a hanging and playful outline so as to shut out the view of the opposite banks thereby giving variety and extent to the whole.
>
> The Plantation on the North and North West of the lake is on rising

ground well calculated for rich ornamental trees, consequently spruce and other Firs were planted intermixed with Oaks, Limes, Elms and Birch trees—but the trees are crowded together leaving only their spindled trunks and unhealthy tops, this incomparable loss has arisen from want of progressive thinning—there is nothing here to meet the eye but bare poles with the exception of a few outside spruce firs adjoining the road—I then examined the Old Wood on the North and West of the House. The House stands on an eminence exposed to the North and West Winds and the Wood had been so placed, no doubt for its protection, which by ordinary thinning and management would have answered that purpose but it is now a mass of bare naked stems carrying poor and unhealthy tops, the Drop from them has destroyed nearly the whole of the Hollies and underwood thereby affording no Screen to the House from the cold and heavy North West Winds. The trees being old and of a great height can only be removed by degrees by weeding the worst out in the first place, affording space for Firs, Hollies, Thorns, Portugal and common Laurels and after they make some progress, then to proceed in like manner, leaving as Standards those where there is any appearance of lateral shoots to branch out, by which means some of the old trees may be preserved and the Plantation thickened—;at the same time it would be advisable now to plant a belt of about 40 yards in width on the outside.

I beg to observe that ground will only produce a certain weight of wood in proportion to its quality, whether in the shape of Hop poles or Timber Trees, and where ornamental wood is required the Hop poles must give way and the ground they occupy for Dwarfs spreading their evergreen foliage over the surface and raising their heads under the arms of the superior trees. Shelter and picturesque and varied forms are in this manner obtained, only let the Standards have sufficient space, nature requires but little assistance.

Dobson concluded his Affidavit by saying that 'Although there are few workmen I should feel inclined to trust with the thinning of ornamental plantations' Coxon, Woodman to the Duke of Portland, could be entrusted with the remedial thinning he recommended.

The result of the case is not known, but Dobson's Affidavit is noteworthy for two qualities characteristic of his life and work—lucidity and commonsense.

There was, in the second quarter of the 19th Century, only one other self-made adventurer in the North, whose boldness of thinking, scale of enterprise and risks taken, exceeded Richard Grainger's. This was George Hudson, (1800-71) 'the Railway King', an ex-draper's assistant from York who, by the mid 1840's, was responsible for operating 1,450 miles of the 5,000 then existing miles of railway and who, to further his schemes, became M.P. for Sunderland for fourteen years from 1845 to 1859 and under whose direction a great part of Sunderland's Dockland was constructed and for whom the beautiful Monkwearmouth Railway Station was built in 1848.

Hudson specialised in building Railways, Grainger in building streets and in rebuilding Newcastle. Both at the successful conclusion of their spectacular enterprises gave banquets for five hundred people or so that lasted for hours, with balls, junketings, and entertainments. Hudson paid dividends out of capital, Grainger built with the money he had just raised on the mortgage of his last building. Hudson lost his shareholders' money, Grainger risked his mortgagees'; Hudson became a millionaire, lost every penny, was publicly disgraced and lived abroad for years to avoid arrest for debt; thanks to John Clayton's untiring efforts, Grainger's financial disaster was kept a secret, and he continued to live, respected and indeed honoured in Newcastle on the £400 a year Clayton's skilful management secured him from his creditors. Hudson returned at last to England and lived on a pension of £600 a year his faithful friends raised for him. Nearly all of Hudson's and Grainger's schemes were proved with the passage of time, to be far-seeing and correct, benefiting their successors, but both men were ruined by them.

Clayton, who in his own affairs was cautious even for an astute attorney, relished risk-taking in others, and appreciated Hudson. Of one of Hudson's Company meetings, when disaster was not far away, Clayton said[44]-

> We all came here with gloomy countenances—we went into the room without at all seeing our way through the night which beset us. —the room was full—all eyes were turned upon my friend, as a quarter from which light would spring upon us. He rose and did not disappoint us—When he had finished speaking no man added one word—We all saw our way. We saw that the thing would be achieved and achieved soon; and we returned to our homes comfortable and Happy.

Even Gladstone, pillar of financial probity, who on many occasions would have been totally aghast at Hudson's methods, said after his exposure and disgrace that he had been 'no mere speculator, but a projector of great discernment, courage, and rich enterprise'.

Hudson was the driving force behind the completion in 1848 of the High Level Bridge which forged the link between Hudson's line from

75

Darlington to Newcastle and Berwick. He formed a Company with George Stephenson as a director and with Robert Stephenson as engineer, but it was Dobson's joint design with Robert Stephenson that gave the bridge its famous outline.

One of Hudson's schemes was to connect his railway system to the little fishing villages of Whiby and Scarborough and to develop Whitby in particular with villas, hotels and all the amenities of a resort for the people of industrial Yorkshire. Hudson chose Dobson to design the main part of his development and the hotels and houses are still there to be seen. There are two particularly fine terraces on Whitby West Cliff but the Royal Crescent is still only half built! There is still a Hudson Street, and although the project was not a financial success for Hudson (too many of the houses failing to sell readily), like so many of his schemes it has proved a success[45] for others. Hudson showed his usual flair in choosing Whitby as his main resort for development. The spectacular, deeply inset harbour surrounded by steep cliffs, with Whitby Abbey and St Mary's Church dominating the highest cliff of all, is a coastal scene which compares with anything in Europe. Hudson plainly decided that the architecture facing Whitby Abbey and the sea should be worthy of its setting.

Dobson's 1857 plan of the intended development confirms what is clear on the ground, that the architecurally most impressive part of the scheme would be that which faced the Abbey and the sea—East Terrace and the Royal Crescent. They were in fact built by Dobson long before his 1857 plan of the 'intended development' was drawn. Hudson bought the West Cliff fields in 1848 and they were built on about 1850. The appearance on Dobson's plan of Hudson Street (quite undistinguished) and the other streets, does not mean that Dobson would design or had then designed them, and only East Terrace and the Royal Crescent can be attributed with confidence to Dobson on stylistic grounds. It is probable that Dobson's plan was designed merely to show the lay out, siting and area of the scheme.

Professor M. G. R. Conzen has drawn attention[46] to the sensitivity with which Dobson 'grafted' the new development on the existing town-scape by 'allowing ample open spaces between the initial East Terrace and the harbour below with its sheltered fringe of fishermen's houses'. Dobson's designs, he says, 'were at once voluminous and impressive with its disciplined rows of three to four-storied and balconied houses lining new streets wider than any Whitby had been used to'.

When Pevsner wrote[47] that the West Cliff development 'has not produced great architecture', his judgement may have been affected by the unsightly modern accretions which, in East Terrace and the Royal Crescent, have partially obscured Dobson's design. Even the fine iron balconies are painted in so many different colours by the individual house owners that the fine sweep of the Terrace and Crescent is lost. But that Royal Crescent, with its alternating classical and curved pedimented windows, and East Terrace with its Royal Hotel, constitute at least architecture of considerable distinction (whether great or not) will, it is hoped be established by the photographs in this book. I find Dobson's Royal Hotel full of hidden distinction—hidden by the shoddy modern entrance with its strip lighting, so that the entry between two Ionic columns can be missed. The ground floor has some fine ceilings, cornices and many Ionic pillars (the upper floors seem to have been stripped of all Dobson decoration), and the dining and reception rooms still retain many Dobson features discernible behind bars or above the gaming machines. This hotel takes its place with the earlier Royal in Scarborough and the first Railway hotels at Charing Cross and St Pancras—palaces designed to give the middle classes on their travels some experience of living with the classical and the sumptuous which the truly rich had long enjoyed. Fine Dobson ironwork with a wreath design (see page 88) at the front of the hotel has been partially removed.

Dobson's views were not all sweetness and light. In his 1859 Presidential Address he declared his surprising (and wrong) view that David Stephenson was not a very good designer—'I will not say that he was an accomplished architect, but he was a man of excellent character and much kindness of disposition'. And in the same address he expressed severe criticism of some of Paine's work. He was so angry when John Johnston's Town Hall was planned to be sited so as to obliterate the view of St. Nicholas, the Castle and Black Gate from the curving Bigg Market, that when asked to advise about some problem posed by the new building his only reply was 'Take the building down'.[48]

When the Northern Architectural Association was formed at a meeting held at The Exchange Hotel, Newcastle upon Tyne, on 13th November 1858, the original twenty-seven members who attended included John Dobson, John Wardle, George Walker, Thomas Oliver,

Thomas Moore of Sunderland, John Green, Thomas Prosser, and J. Johnston. Dobson was elected their first President.

Although he was now over seventy, he was as busy as ever, still rising early and working late to get the detail correct. His last commission was for the Earl of Durham for the new front and Great Hall of Lambton Castle, which had only been saved from collapse many years previously by his ingenuity. The Great Hall was 94 feet high, 76 feet long and 64 feet wide. The design, said his daughter, 'was worthy of a feudal prince'. Dobson never saw this commission finished but after his death it was carried to completion by his son-in-law Sydney Smirke R.A.

In 1863 Dobson was stricken by a stroke which left him partly paralysed and from which he never really recovered, although in the two years that remained to him hopes of recovery were never abandoned. He kept on the house at 15 New Bridge Street, Newcastle, but moved to a house in Ryton where it was hoped the country air and surroundings would benefit him. Between 1863 and his death, his commissions were completed by other architects and he was never active in practice again.

At the end of December 1864 he was weakening and returned with his daughter to 15 New Bridge Street, Newcastle where he died on Sunday, 8th January, 1865 aged seventy-seven. The *Newcastle Daily Chronicle* on 9th January 1865 referred to his outstanding contribution to the architecture of the North, and his 'robust powerful frame which enabled him in after years to do the work of three ordinary men, and a hearty genial temper and straightforward honesty of conduct which cleared his professional course of many obstacles and made friends with all he came in contact—few men have spent so long a life in so laborious a manner and made so few enemies'.

He was buried in the Jesmond Cemetery he had designed and planted. John Clayton was one of the pall bearers with Sidney Smirke. His New Bridge Street House is now part of the site of a dance-hall and is known as "The Dobson suite",—a memorial as singularly inappropriate as that the new street recently named after him should be the ugliest street ever built in the city. He left a comfortable sum of just under £16,000, and there is no reason to doubt his daughter's statement that he never exceeded an estimate and never had a legal dispute with a contractor'.

The Royal Arcade, Newcastle upon Tyne. Watercolour by John Dobson. (*Laing Art Gallery*)
(Demolished in the 1960's as part of the 'development' plan)

Eldon Square, Newcastle upon Tyne, 1824
(Now demolished)

Dobson's original design in watercolour for the Central Station, Newcastle upon Tyne, showing external and internal double colonnades and an Italianate tower at the east end. (*Laing Art Gallery*)

Dobson's Central Station Portico, built under the supervision of Thomas Prosser, the Railway Company's architect in 1836 when Dobson had retired from practice after a stroke. (*Ursula Clark*) Below: detail after cleaning (*Newcastle Chronicle & Journal*)

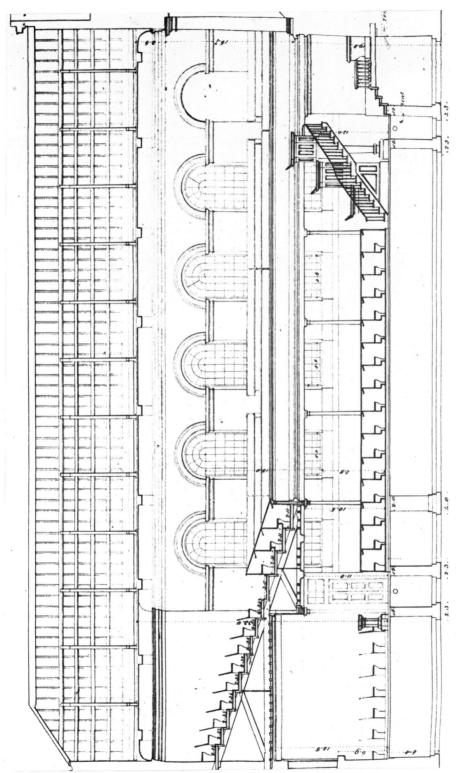

Above and following page: Dobson's design for the proposed Church of St John, Elswick, 1841. The elevation is rendered in watercolour. (*By courtesy of Newcastle University Librarian*)

Dobson's watercolour of St. Thomas' Church, Newcastle upon Tyne, designed 1825, consecrated 1830.
(*Laing Art Gallery*)

Interior of Clayton Memorial Church, Jesmond, Newcastle upon Tyne —
designed 1858, consecrated 1861. (*Ken Hitcham, Philipson Studios*)

The Royal Crescent, Whitby, by John Dobson. 1850–1852. (*Photograph by Thomas Watson of Whitby 1898*)
(*By courtesy of John Tindale Esq.*)

The Royal Hotel, Whitby, by John Dobson

Ironwork railings outside Royal Hotel, Whitby, designed by Dobson
(Photographs, John Tindale, Whitby)

Portrait of George Hudson (1806 – 1871) M.P. for Sunderland (1845 – 1859) by
Francis Grant *(By courtesy of the Tyne and Wear Museums Committee)*

89

DOBSON ROOFS

The Royal Arcade, Newcastle upon Tyne, showing roof arches springing from the tops of the great pilasters with arches and domes decorated with ironwork tracery. (Demolished and reconstructed, mainly in fibreglass, within Swan House).

DOBSON ROOFS
Timber roof above the arcaded Butcher Market

91

DOBSON ROOFS
Clayton Memorial Church, Jesmond, the roof
(*Ken Hitcham, Philipson Studios*)

92

DOBSON ROOFS

The Vegetable Market with timber roof and ironwork columned supports

DOBSON ROOFS

Newcastle Central Station roof with curved iron ribs each 60 feet in length forming the principal arches of the curving roof — the first use of curved, rolled iron ribbing for roofing and a Dobson invention. (See Appendix 1)

Grey Street, Newcastle upon Tyne planned by Richard Grainger and built to the designs of architects who were all influenced by Dobson. The building with a portico is The Theatre Royal by John and Benjamin Green, 1837, and the adjoining building on the left is Lloyds (originally Lambton's) Bank from Grainger's own office. The lower end of Grey Street on the left (East) side was by Dobson himself. The West side of the street was designed by various other architects working with Grainger.

POSTSCRIPT

Time has not treated Dobson's work kindly, although outside Newcastle his main achievement remains intact.

In Newcastle, even in the last fifteen years, his Royal Arcade, Eldon Square, and 41 Blackett Street (formerly T. M. Richardson's Northern Academy of Art) has been demolished. Only the strenuous efforts of the Victorian Society and finally ministerial intervention saved from destruction Dobson's Cemetery Gates and Lodges at Jesmond, described by J. C. Loudon as the most appropriate entrance to a cemetery he knew.[49] Grainger's first graceful street of Georgian architecture, Higham Place, is mutilated, three quarters demolished, and reduced to a rump. A 17th Century inn of great quality was not spared.

The destruction of Eldon Square represented a double blow to Dobson's work in Newcastle—first the actual destruction of the work itself, and secondly the threat that the unlovely transformation of the Square into a vast 'shopping precinct' carries to the prosperity and continued occupation of the shops in the older streets of Newcastle designed by Dobson, Wardle and Walker and built by Grainger.

The unholy trinity that has done so much damage to so many cities—Comprehensive Redevelopment, Rateable Value and the Motor Car, has deprived Newcastle of many of its best buildings and much of its character.

What Newcastle has been given in exchange for its older buildings is not architecture at all but building construction—a very different thing. Dobson would have agreed with Sir Edwin Lutyens that 'Architecture begins where function ends'. Unless there is a change of attitude in England to the preservation of old buildings and a new scrupulousness in the design and the materials used in new building, architecture as Sir Edwin Lutyens defined it and Dobson practised it will become a thing of the past.

Nothing reflects the spirit of an age more truthfully than its architecture—except perhaps its coinage which also cannot hide debasement. Visiting a great house by Dobson and seeing the confidence and wealth and belief in the future of which it is an expression, one is compelled to realise that its spirit is as alien to our present age as are the Pyramids. The truth is that the more equal the society the worse its architecture will be.

Jesmond Cemetery showing the original landscaping
(*Engraving by W. Collard*)

APPENDIX ONE

ADDRESS

TO THE MEMBERS OF THE

NORTHERN

ARCHITECTURAL ASSOCIATION.

BY

JOHN DOBSON, ESQ., F.I.B.A.,
PRESIDENT.

READ AT THE FIRST QUARTERLY MEETING.
HELD APRIL 19, 1859.

GENTLEMEN — This being the first quarterly meeting of the Northern Architectural Society, as you have done me the honour of electing me your President, I will take the liberty of addressing to you a few introductory observations. I can truly say that I view this meeting, and the establishment of this Society, with much of that anxious feeling with which the agriculturist regards the sowing of his spring seed, hoping that, by the assistance of Divine Providence, and by a united and friendly feeling towards each other, we may look back upon the auspicious occasion of our present meeting with pride and satisfaction. If our proceedings are attended with all the advantages which I anticipate, they will greatly tend to promote a desire to follow our pursuits with strict adherence to professional honour; avoiding in all our transactions those petty jealousies which are so unbecoming in men of a liberal profession, and leaving the public to estimate our value without having recourse to self-praise, which is not only calculated to bring ridicule on the individual, but is derogatory to the character of the profession, which it should be our chief aim to elevate.

I will now proceed, gentlemen, to take a glance at the progress of architecture during the present century, more particularly with reference to the Northern Counties of England. The architectural student of the present day, I may premise, has numerous advantages which did not exist in former years. About 50 years ago there were but few publications on architecture, and such as existed were, with very few exceptions, the work of very indifferent authors, and still more indifferent artists. There were very few works of any authority on either ecclesiastical or domestic architecture until the time of Pugin; while now we are inundated by illustrated works of the highest value and importance, and periodical works devoted to our art, and conducted by men of ability, abound not only in our own country, but come to us also from the ablest writers and artists of France and Germany. In addition to these sources of information, we have numerous admirable papers, written by men of talent and experience, read at the meetings of the various societies established in London, Edinburgh, and elsewhere. These, gentlemen, are advantages, and sources of information and improvement, which it is impossible too highly to appreciate. The facilities afforded now to all of visiting foreign countries, are also advantages of inestimable value, which our predecessors were without. The student has an opportunity of sketching for himself the best examples of his art, which formerly he could know only through prints or drawings little to be relied on.

It is by actual personal observation only that lasting impressions of outline and detail can be acquired. I cannot too strongly urge the younger men in our profession to seek for information by a personal inspection of those works which are calculated to quicken the judgment and improve the taste, whether they may be in our own country or on the Continent, in many parts of which our art has been far longer and more munificently encouraged than here. Ours is a profession in which no one should

John Dobson in middle age (*Northern Architectural Association archive, by courtesy of RIBA Northern Region*)

consider his education completed, however elaborately he may have studied his art. We should never cease our studies, or be satisfied with the amount of knowledge we may have acquired. A remark addressed to me by West, the Royal Academician, when at the age of eighty-two, made a strong impression on my mind. "When a man," said he, "ceases to consider himself a pupil, he must be retrograding in his profession." West at that time was engaged on his last picture, "Death on the Pale Horse," and was then studying from nature with all the energy of youth. If I may be allowed the privilege of old men to speak of myself, I would say, that although myself approaching towards the age of West, I still can feel the same anxiety to improve, and the same pleasure and delight in my profession that I felt when I was but a boy. Human life is too limited, whatever amount of talent and industry may be employed, to arrive at anything much beyond mediocrity, and therefore it behoves us, if we love our profession, to make the most of our time. You may rely upon it that such a course tends greatly to increase our happiness; for there is no profession that affords more intellectual and healthy enjoyment than ours. He who has not such feelings within him, must find his avocation one of labour and drudgery, instead of delight; and, for his own sake, it were better that he should at once take up some new pursuit.

On comparing the present with the past state of our profession, it is a great source of gratification to mark the great advances that have been made. Whether we look to London, the artistic, as well as the political head of the country, or to the provinces, we shall find immense strides have been made in art. Since the termination of the great European war, in 1815, our country has vastly increased in wealth and commercial importance, and, as a natural consequence, leisure has been afforded to direct men's attention to the study and encouragement of the arts and sciences. To correct and improve the taste of the people, large sums of money are annually appropriated by Parliament for the support of public institutions calculated to promote that end. The magnificent collections at the British Museum, at the National Gallery, at South Kensington—the Schools of Design all over the country—the various local museums, galleries, and lecture rooms—all are indications of the growing taste of the people, and of the wise policy of the Government in encouraging that taste. The munificence of enlightened individuals has greatly promoted these objects; and I cannot refrain from pointing to the School of Design at Alnwick, established by our Northumbrian duke, as a noble instance of such liberality. Let me here point proudly to our own Society of Architects, in which already are enrolled about thirty members, as an unmistakable evidence of our great social and æsthetic progress.

Since the commencement of the present century, architecture in the Northern Counties has, I think, been somewhat in advance of most other districts. Fifty years ago there was no employment for a professional architect; the duties were performed by builders alone, who united to their special business the profession of an architect. As a proof of the talent of some of these builders, I may refer you to All Saints' Church, designed by Mr. D. Stephenson; and to the elegant proportions of the tower and spire, as a proof of his taste and skill. At the same period Mr. Newton practised as a builder and architect; he both designed and executed the Assembly Rooms of this town; Backworth House, Northumberland; and other country houses of minor importance. Then followed Mr. Stokoe, who also practised in the various capacities of architect, surveyor, and builder; he designed Elswick Hall, Newcastle, and Harton House, Northumberland; and in conjunction with his son William, was architect, contractor, and builder of the County Courts in this town. These were men of talent, whose works might have been an ornament to the country, had they fortunately been better educated in their profession.

It may not, perhaps, be uninteresting to you, gentlemen, if I pursue this inquiry, and cast a rapid glance over the course of our profession since the period to which I have been adverting. I cannot, however, in this address, venture to notice the great advance that has been made in our street architecture. This would occupy too much of our time; and the omission may, perhaps, be the more readily excused, as you yourselves have witnessed the erection of those magnificent buildings in Newcastle, which owe, in a great measure, their origin to the spirit and enterprise of Mr. Grainger.

At the early period to which I have adverted, fifty years ago, Mr. Stephenson, whom I have just named in connection with the elegant structure, All Saints' Church, was the sole practitioner in Newcastle as an architect, and it was in his office that I completed my clerkship in 1809. I will not say that he was an accomplished architect, but he was a man of excellent character and much kindness of disposition. It was by his counsel and advice that I resolved, when leaving him, to establish myself as a professional architect. I need hardly say that I found, what many other young men have found, that it was far easier to profess an art than to practise it. The services of an architect were then but little in request, and you will readily suppose that to one so young, so inexperienced, so unknown, engagements came in like angel's visits. But how hidden to us are the ways of Providence! It was probably to this very circumstance that I owe my present position in our profession. Want of sufficient employment gave me leisure, and leisure gave me the opportunity of acquiring far more professional knowledge than I could acquire in Mr. Stephenson's office. I employed a great portion of my time in travelling, sketching, and studying the higher branches of the art. At this period my old and worthy friend Bonomi practised as an architect in Durham; he was the surveyor of the county. It is true that, like myself, he had little or no practice, but he and I enjoyed the somewhat barren dignity of being at that time the only professional architects in the counties of Northumberland and Durham.

At the period of which I am reverting, our northern towns were free from smoke, and not considered objectionable places of residence for persons of the better or wealthier class. The immediate vicinity of Newcastle was surrounded with pleasant and romantic walks. The banks of the river Tyne, from Newcastle to Shields, a distance of about eight miles, were well covered with magnificent hanging woods, enriched with flowering shrubs to the water's edge, presenting to the youthful mind a picture little short of Paradise; but how has the scene changed! Now, in those pleasant places we find extensive manufactures, blast furnaces, chemical works, cinder ovens, wood and iron ship-building; and in place of the humble passenger-boat, or wherry, we see a fleet of steamers and tug-boats, with a dark and gloomy atmosphere from the dense smoke suspended over the entire district. The stunning and terrific noise from the steam hammer, the hollow and unearthly bellowings of the blast furnace, and the stench from the sulphurous combinations at the numerous alkali works, lead us to think that the fallen angels have taken up their abode on this spot, and instead of Paradise we might fancy ourselves in the dominions of Satan. But as a compensation for the loss of the romantic walk, the wild rose, and the delightful woodbine, we have the satisfaction of finding our working population better fed and employed, the merchant, manufacturer, coalowner, and shipowner enriched, and the wealthy seeking a pleasant retreat in those fertile parts of the country which the hand of the spoiler has not yet reached. It is here that the architect is required to erect elegant and costly mansions, whilst in the towns have arisen capacious public buildings, improved street architecture, and a better class of dwellings for the working community; the progress and completion of railways have also called into requisition the engineer and architect, in the erection of railway stations, bridges, and stupendous viaducts, rivalling those of ancient Rome.

I will now, gentlemen, by your leave, make a few observations on the domestic architecture of the higher classes of our country gentlemen. Among those who embellished the country with noble works of architecture at the earlier part of the last century, Sir John Vanbrough stands pre-eminent. Undoubtedly he was a man of no common genius. In his exterior architecture, boldness and originality distinguished him from all his contemporaries. His style was founded on the Italian, but in his efforts to produce a striking effect by picturesque outline and breadth of light and shade, he cared little about the minor elegancies of Italian art, and indeed degenerated sometimes into grotesqueness. His interiors were grand, and full of display, to suit the gay and voluptuous manners of the times; these objects he effected to a very high degree, but they were accomplished at the sacrifice of convenience and comfort; instances of which may be seen at Seaton Delaval, Castle Howard, and Blenheim. Sir John's general plan was to enter the building direct from the north, into a magnificent hall, with corridors leading right and left; the consequence was, that the current of air from the exterior was unchecked, and rendered the building in cold weather almost uninhabitable. The late Lord Strathmore, who was a constant visitor at Seaton Delaval, complained to me of the want of comfort in the house, and that he felt obliged always to have an extra cloak with him when residing there. When the property became Sir Jacob Astley's, I was engaged to restore the house, and I do not remember ever feeling comfortable in any of the apartments, not even at the dinner table. The capacious and hospitable fire-place of Sir Jacob's dining-room served but to quicken the currents of cold air that found their way through the ample avenues of that noble but comfortless abode.

After Sir John Vanbrough, Mr. Payne was the architect most employed in the north of England. Mr. Payne designed Belford House, Gosforth, Axwell Park, and Bywell. In his designs he usually made the entrance of his mansions at the south, entering direct into a hall, and

105

from thence to a staircase, providing no check to the rush of air from the main door. Payne, therefore, effected little or no improvement on his predecessor in the interior temperature of houses. Moreover, by making his entrance on the side where the best aspect is usually obtained, he prevented the ground from being properly planted, so as to afford the necessary shelter, and deprived the building of the advantages of rich and full-dressed ground about the house. Mr. Payne was unfortunately considered a great authority, and consequently, all the houses built in the north of England were mere copies of Mr. Payne's general plan. An architect, indeed, became a superfluous luxury. When a gentleman wanted a house erected, all he had to do was to inform the builder of the size of the rooms required, the plan being a small entrance hall on the south, the staircase opposite, the dining room on one side and the drawing-room on the other, with the library, &c., behind. We thus see how much mischief an incompetent man may do, if he be but favoured by fortune and fashion; not only do his patrons suffer, but an example is set by which mischief is perpetuated. Even to this day the evil example is not entirely obliterated, and we may still meet with men who, preferring the beaten track to the dictates of common sense, will starve their patrons, because their fathers were starved before them. Our friends from the south find too often occasion to complain of the cold blasts with which we are apt to receive them. The subject is, I think, one well deserving the attention of the members of this Association. The defects I have named ought to be obviated; and allow me to recommend to you to endeavour as much as possible to produce at all times a uniform temperature in every building. I have designed many mansions of various sizes in different parts of England, and one of my first objects has been so to plan the house that I might have the entrance where it is least commanding in its view; this affords me an opportunity of planting out the entrance front, so that the strong winds are checked as much as possible; whilst, in planning my interior, I always consider it of primary importance to prevent direct currents of air from entering and passing through the house.

In reference to the most appropriate style of exterior for the class of mansions to which I am alluding, so much depends upon situation, surrounding scenery, and other circumstances, that I cannot venture upon this matter at the present time, for the subject is too important to be treated incidentally.

The time that I devoted to the study of castellated architecture was considered by many of my friends as a great loss, as it was not likely that I should be called upon to erect many buildings of that class, particularly as such a style was considered ill adapted in every respect for domestic comfort. But no sooner had I spent three months at Conway, Carnarvon, and Beaumaris, Wales (where, in my opinion, are some of the finest examples of castellated architecture in the kingdom), than designs were required for the erection of county prisons, court-house, &c., for Northumberland. A design, which I submitted in competition with others, was accepted—a distinction of which I was not a little proud, for I was at that time very young and little known to the public. I then found that the knowledge I had gained of castellated architecture was invaluable to me, not only in the construction of Morpeth gaol, but in many other instances where I have been called upon to alter castellated buildings already erected, and where I have had abundant opportunities to avail myself of my studies among the old castles. You see, then, what advantage a student derives from earnestly availing himself of every opportunity that offers of acquiring professional knowledge; and if any of you desire it, I shall be happy at any time to show you my sketches of old castles.

But, to continue: The extension of the old castle, with its small loop-holes and its large surface of blank wall, is, it must be admitted, not an interesting object to the eye, but that expression of strength and heaviness arose out of necessity; light and healthy chambers could only be obtained where the apartments overlooked the interior courts; hence arose the many beautiful examples we have of oriel and other projecting windows, commanding distant views over the embattled walls and barbicans. As a proof of a partiality to lightness of interior construction, I have only to refer you to the beautiful chapels at Conway and Beaumaris.

Whilst studying and sketching examples of Tudor architecture, I found that interior convenience was alone the object sought to be accomplished, and that much of the picturesque effect arose from chance. Much might be said of the advantages of Tudor architecture in the construction of buildings for domestic purposes, in producing varied and picturesque outlines, when the forms appear to arise out of necessity; and I do not see that there can be any objection to adopting the decorated style of detail to a Tudor outline, provided it harmonises with the building. When this style is found to be too costly, then I have found what may be called the Manor House style, or irregular outline, a good substitute; and in some cases it will be found more in harmony with the component parts of the landscape. Many excellent examples of buildings of this class have been erected of late years.

On the subject of ecclesiastical architecture, and its progress in this country, I would observe that the beginning of the present century might be called the dark age, for no architect had courage to attempt anything like purity of Gothic; and it was only after it became fashionable among a portion of the clergy that an architect was permitted to introduce a Gothic design; hence we are much indebted to the societies of Oxford and Cambridge, who introduced the custom of clerical gentleman devoting a portion of their time to the study of ecclesiastical architecture. Time will not permit me to dilate upon this subject; but it is a fertile one, and I trust I may be permitted at some future time to address you upon it.

Now, with respect to the construction of buildings erected in the North of England about fifty years ago, I may remark that the whole of the execution was rude and unmechanical. The first step to improvement was introduced by Sir Charles Monck, when he commenced building Belsay Castle—a mansion designed and constructed after classic models. Sir Charles had resided and studied for some time in Greece, and having a refined taste, and mechanical talent, he made the masonry of his new house equal to any of the polished marble temples of that classic land; this at once introduced a style of masonry previously unknown, and those who could afford the expense soon followed his example. I consider that the North of England is much indebted to the worthy baronet's enterprise and cultivated taste. The masons employed at Belsay Castle, on completing their work, branched off into different parts of England, and since that time a Northumbrian mason has been considered amongst the best that could be found in any part of the country.

Many of our best houses have suffered very much from the exterior part of the foundation and cellar walls being filled in with the soil taken from the excavations. The walls consequently are kept in moisture, thereby creating a constant damp or vapour beneath the floors. This defect was readily overcome, by placing a slight wall a few inches from the foundations, covering the vent, on a level with the surface of the ground, with dressed stone or flags, perforated so as to admit a thorough ventilation entirely round the exterior of the building. Since I adopted this plan I have never known an instance of dry rot to take place. With respect to battening walls for the purpose of obviating moisture, it was the practice in Mr. Payne's time, not only to batten the external but also the interior walls; in the event of fire, however, this plan was found to be extremely dangerous, and was the cause of the destruction of Hexham Abbey House. In opening out the Roman baths at Holton Castle, on the estate of Sir Edward Blackett, Bart., Northumberland, I found that the Romans had lined their walls with tiles about 9 inches by 15, each side of the tile returning about an inch, thus producing a current of air and preventing the moisture from penetrating into the interior. The tiles were fixed to the stone walls by T headed nails, some of which I found quite perfect. From this time I adopted the example thus set us by the Romans, using bricks in the same manner as they used their tiles, and leaving a space of about two inches between the stone walls and bricks.

In the early years of my practice, good carpentry was also but little understood; so that if a builder had to place a roof on a building, say 50 or 60 feet square, the plan was to make one main principal of great strength, and to trim the hip and other principals into it, thereby laying the main weight of the roof on the centre portion of the structure. I had not been long in practice, however, before I discovered the defects of this plan, which I easily obviated by trussing the purlings, which are now called diminished principals, each answering as a purling, and creating a regular pressure on each side of the building. Hence arose my idea of trussing roofs. In my design of the Newcastle markets, the same construction may be seen in the capacious roof in the vegetable department. Many improvements in other branches of carpentry have taken place within late years, and the subject is one well deserving of further consideration.

The facility of obtaining malleable iron led me to originate a new style of roofing for the Central Station, Newcastle, which I effected by introducing curved principals. This was not accomplished, however, without much anxiety and consideration, as the rolling mills at that time only supplied flat plates of iron, out of which the curved rafters had to be cut; this increased the expense so much, that at one time I did not find myself justified in introducing them; but by a simple contrivance of bevelled rollers, regulated to suit the curve of the principals, the expense was reduced to the extent of £1,400 in the roof alone of the station.

I may here, perhaps, appropriately make allusion to the heavy weight of responsibility which rests upon an architect, particularly in the department of construction. The contractor, we find, is only responsible for the proper supply of such materials and labour as specified, or as may be reasonably inferred from the constructive drawings and specifications, and other directions of the architect. The contractor's responsibility, therefore, ceases after the approval of the architect or clerk of the works; but the architect is responsible on failure of construction, when he is remunerated by commission and not by time. Where difficult foundations have to be encountered, such as the foundation for the railway warehouses at the Manors, across Pandon Dean, Newcastle, which was at the time only town deposit, and of a depth of 50 to 60 feet, and that for the most part in a state of fermentation, it may be conceived how heavy are the responsibilities of an architect, and what care and judgment are required in such a case as I have named to form a suitable foundation, and to provide for a reasonable settlement of the building. This, I may observe, was done in erecting these warehouses, by concrete footings, varying in width from 6 to 14 feet, in proportion to the weight of the superstructure, the settlement not exceeding 7 in. over the whole. Who then can say that an architect who has to encounter so much anxiety, and is subject to so many risks, in designing ornamental buildings of a limited size, is overpaid by the ordinary commission of 5 per cent.? Therefore, in designing new works, or in preparing plans for the alteration of old ones, it behoves us to proceed with caution and judgment.

I have now, gentlemen, occupied as much of your time as is usually allotted to the delivery of an ordinary address. To treat the different subjects in detail, to which I have alluded, would, you are aware, occupy many evenings. I have therefore, preferred taking a general view of the state of architecture in this district, as I have known it during my own practice only, introducing such few observations as the occasion seemed to justify. I hope the subject will be considered of sufficient interest by other members to induce them to favour the Society with their views at future meetings. Whilst by the formation of this Society we are endeavouring to elevate the profession, and to establish a uniformity of practice, we have, at the same time, afforded to us an opportunity of intercourse in reference to matters of difficulty and doubt that may arise in the course of practice. In thanking you for the patient attention with which you have favoured me, I assure you that I shall be happy to refer to examples in greater detail, and give any further information that may be desired with reference to the sketches I have now the pleasure of placing before you.

APPENDIX TWO

A LIST OF JOHN DOBSON'S WORK

Because of the rarity of Dobson's plans and drawings, this list of his work is necessarily based largely on the list set out in Margaret Jane Dobson's 1885 *Memoir*. I have corrected the obvious errors in her list and claims which seem to be contradicted by the contemporary evidence or later discoveries, qualified by my own research and reference to the works of Pevsner and H. M. Colvin.[50]

Although reference has been made to the inaccuracy of Miss Dobson's list, it remains true that anyone interested in the architecture of the 19th Century is much in her debt. It would have been extremely difficult for anyone to-day to compile a comprehensive list of John Dobson's work without her attempt to do so.

It is hoped that as a result of this book further information will come to light, especially as to the exact alterations or restoration work done to buildings not originally designed by Dobson. In addition to deleting what seemed to be inaccuracies and revising the list generally (no doubt adding errors of my own) I have in certain cases amplified Miss Dobson to bring reference up to date. The appearance of an asterisk before the name of a building signifies that the building has been demolished, although the absence of an asterisk should not be taken as proof that the building still stands. The Pevsner quotations and page references included in the list are from his book *The Buildings of Northumberland*, and I am grateful to Penguin books for permission to include them and to John Murray for permission to include references from H. M. Colvin's *Biographical Dictionary of British Architects*, (2nd edition, 1978).

DOMESTIC ARCHITECTURE

Designed Residence of J. Nicholson Esq., North Seaton, Earsdon, Northumberland, 1813.[50]

111

Large Additions to Gibside House, Northumberland, for Lord Strathmore, 1813, 1815, 1856.
(The house is now a ruin, Dobson's drawings for additions to Gibside are in Durham County records office Colvin p. 268).

Large alterations to Bradley Hall, for Lord Ravensworth, 1813.

Designed Field House, Gateshead on Tyne, 1813.

Planned very large additions to Wynyard, Durham, Seat of Marquis of Londonderry, ("apparently not executed", says Colvin, like Dobson's plans for New Town and Harbour at Seaham for Lord Londonderry) 1815 and 1845.
Designed Residence of R. Rippon Esq., Waterville, North Shields, 1815.

Additions to Falloden Hall, Northumberland, Seat of Sir George Grey, Bart., 1815.
(Gutted by Fire and rebuilt this Century)

Designed Prestwick Lodge, Near Ponteland, Residence of Percival Fenwick Esq., 1815.

Restored west wing of Vanbrughs Seaton Delaval, Northumberland, Destroyed by fire in 1752 for Sir Jacob Astley, Bart., 1815.
(The centre of the building was destroyed by fire in 1822).

Large additions to Unthank Hall, Northumberland, Seat of Dixon Dixon, Esq., 1815 and 1860.

Designed Birtley Hall, County Durham, for J. Warwick Esq., 1815.

*Designed Benwell Grove, Newcastle-on-Tyne, the Property of Charles Cook, Esq., 1816. (Demolished)

Large Additions to Minsteracres, Northumberland, Seat of George Silvertopp, Esq., 1816.

Designed Eland Hall, Ponteland, Northumberland, William Barkley, Esq., 1816.

Designed Residence of J. Errington, Esq., Whickham-on-Tyne, 1816.

Alterations and Additions to Paine's Axwell Park, for Sir John Clavering, Bart., 1817.

*Designed Jesmond Grove for James Losh, Esq., Jesmond, Newcastle-on-Tyne, 1817. (Demolished).

Designed Villa Real now called Nazareth House, Newcastle-on-Tyne, Residence of Captain Dutton, 1817. (Four Tuscan columns at entrance Portico with big bow window at front. Hall with iron balustraded staircase up 3 sides and glass dome over. All the essential Dobson elements.)

Additions to Jesmond House, Newcastle, Residence of Armorer Donkin, Esq., 1818.

Very Extensive Additions to Doxford House, Northumberland, Seat of William Taylor, Esq., 1818. (Now an Old People's Home).

Alterations to Paine's Belford Hall, Northumberland, Seat of William Clark, Esq., 1818. (A noble mansion now sadly neglected)

Additions to Paine's Gosforth Hall, Newcastle-on-Tyne, for the Brandling Family, 1818.

Restored Chipchase Castle, 1819.

Large Additions to Cheesburn Grange, Northumberland, for Ralph Riddell, Esq., 1813 and 1819.
Dobson designed the chapel in 1813, moved the front door of the house from the South to the West front, added the Tower over the front door, refaced the South front, altering the windows and adding the parapet. Hanson in 1860 added a Gothic East wing demolished in 1973. This consisted of a high block comprising Dining Room with Bedroom above and a single storey extension, and Pevnser thinks the Chapel was designed by Hanson at this date. Dobson's daughter hints that the 1813 plans and drawings were not implemented until 1841, and states that the Chapel was not built until 1852 by Dobson. But the Owners of Cheesburn think the Chapel was built when the major remodelling of the house was done by Dobson in 1813.

Designed Residence of John Fenwick Esq., North Shields, 1819.

Restored Rock Hall, Northumberland 1819 for Charles Bosanquet Esq., I am indebted to Dr. Charles Bosanquet, the present owner of Rock for the information that the family belief has always been that Dobson began to restore Rock Hall in about 1819 and not in 1845 as stated in Margaret Jane Dobson's list. That the Bosanquet family tradition is correct is proved by a reference Dr. Bosanquet discovered in the "History, Directory and Gazateer of the Counties of Durham and Northumberland" published in 1828 which states, "Rock Hall has been repaired, enlarged and beautified by its present owner and the remaining part of the old mansion has an impressive and venerable appearance". What is almost certainly Dobson's work is the addition to the pele tower on the south front of two hexagonal wings, two stories high, a drawing room and library on the ground floor and bedrooms above, with a range of stables. A coach house was also built.

Altered Hexham Abbey House, 1819.
After fire damage for T. R. Beaumont Esq.

Alterations to the Hermitage, Hexham, Residence of R. L. Allgood Esq., 1819. Alterations to Hebburn Hall, for Cuthbert Ellison Esq., 1819.

Designed Chirton House, North Shields, Residence of Michael Robson, Esq., 1819.

Alterations to *Broome Park, Northumberland. Seat of William Burrell, Esq., 1820.
(House demolished before 1969. House on site is remodelled Stable Block).

Added to *Biddlestone, Northumberland. Seat of Walter Selby, Esq., 1820. (Demolished during the 1960s).

Some Restorations at Aydon Castle, Northumberland, for Sir Edward Blackett, Bart., 1820.
(Empty but now being restored by the Department of the Environment).

Designed Hawthorn Dene House, Seaham, Durham, for Major Anderson, 1821.

Designed Newbrough Hall, Northumberland, for Rev. H. Wastell, 1821.
(A Classical House with Central Pediment).

Designed South Hill House, Chester-le-Street, for Thomas Fenwick, Esq., 1821.

Designed Black Dene House, (Jesmond Dene House), for Dr. Headlam, 1822.

Designed Angerton House, Northumberland (in the Tudor Style with large Gothic Hall). Seat of Ralph Atkinson, Esq., 1823.

Designed Mitford Hall, Northumberland, Residence of Bertram Osbaldiston Mitford, Esq., 1823. (Built in 1828).

Designed *Swansfield House, Near Alnwick, Residence of H. C. Selby, Esq., 1823. (Demolished 1973).

Additions to the Towers, Jesmond, Newcastle, Residence of Burdon Sanderson, Esq., 1823 to 1827. (Now La Sagesse School).

Designed Residence of Rev. H. Hollingsworth, Haltwhistle, Northumberland, 1823.

Designed Sittringham House, Yorkshire, 1824.

Designed Nunnykirk, Northumberland, (A Classical Masterpiece). Seat of William Ord, Esq., 1825. (Now a school).

Designed Gortanloisk, Argyllshire, for Sir John Fife, 1827.

Alterations to Rickman's Matfen Hall, Matfen, Northumberland, Seat of Sir Edward Blackett, Bart., 1828. (Now a Cheshire Home).

Designed Lilburn Tower, Northumberland, Seat of Henry Collingwood, Esq., 1828.
(This house has only recently ceased to be occupied by members of the family who commissioned Dobson).

Designed Longhirst, Northumberland, Seat of William Lawson, Esq., 1828. (Now a school).

Designed Residence of Charles Bruce, Esq., Edinburgh, 1828.

Alterations to Woolsington Hall, Northumberland, Residence of Matthew Bell, Esq., 1828.

Alterations to Harbottle House, Northumberland, Seat of Thomas Fenwicke Clennell, Esq., 1829.

Alterations to Ridley Hall, Northumberland, Residence of John Davison, Esq., 1829.

Additions to Glanton Park, Northumberland, Residence of Henry Collingwood, Esq., 1829.

Designed Trewhitt House, Rothbury, Northumberland, Residence of J. Smart, Esq., 1830.

Rebuilt Benwell Tower, Newcastle-on-Tyne, Residence of Thomas Crawhall, Esq., 1830. (Became in 1882 the Residence of the Bishop of Newcastle. It is now a Night Club).

Designed Brinkburn Grange, Northumberland, Seat of Major Cadogan. Designed 1830, completed 1837. (Dobson built a new West wing with Entrance Portico on to an older House to the East. On the original East side of the house he inserted a huge bow with 6 Georgian-Gothic windows).

Designed Meldon, Northumberland, Seat of Isaac Cookson, Esq., 1832.

Added to the Chesters, Residence of John Clayton, Esq., 1832 and 1837. (This is the 18th Century house where John Clayton lived until his death on 14th July 1890 at the age of ninety eight. It was enlarged and re-modelled by Norman Shaw in 1891 whose re-interpretation of the 18th Century shows a refinement absent from Cragside).

Large Additions to Blenkinsop, Northumberland. Residence of Colonel Coulson, 1832 and 1837.

Designed *Neasham Hall, Co. Durham as Seat for Colonel Cookson, 1834 completed 1837. (Demolished 1970 by Sir John Wrightson who built a smaller house on site).

Designed Residence of J. Wilson, Esq., Darlington, 1834.

Alterations to the Vicarage, Stamfordham, 1834.

Built Chatton Vicarage, 1834. (Incorporating a Pele Tower).

Additions to High Warden, Northumberland Residence of John Errington, Esq., 1834.

Designed Beaufront Castle, on the Tyne, Seat of William Cuthbert, Esq., 1835 completed 1841.

Designed Holme Eden, Near Carlisle, Residence of Peter Dixon, Esq., 1837.

Restored *Swinburne Castle, Northumberland, Residence of Thomas Riddell, Esq., 1840. (The present owner Mr. John Riddell has no knowledge of any work done by Dobson, and since the castle was considerably added to in about 1780 is doubtful whether it would need any restoration work in 1840. The main house was demolished in the 1960s).

Designed Moor House, Sunderland, 1840.

Alterations to East Boldon House, Durham, Residence of William Gray, Esq., 1840.

Restoration work to Bamburgh Castle, Northumberland, 1843.

Alterations to Hartburn Vicarage, 1843.

Designed The Hags, now called Hackwood, Hexham, Residence of Charles Head, Esq., 1843.

Restored Haughton Castle, North Tyne, Residence of William Smith, Esq., 1844.

Alterations to Settrington Rectory, East Riding, Yorkshire, an 18th Century house, 1845.

Designed Residence of H. Harrison, Esq., Linethwaite near Whitehaven, Cumberland, 1845.

Altered the Knells, Near Carlisle, Residence of John Dixon, Esq., 1845.

Designed Cleadon Cottage, Near Sunderland, Residence of Robert Swinburne, Esq., 1845.

Designed Bank House, Newbiggin, Residence of J. H. Hinde, Esq., 1845. (Now a Working Men's Club)

Designed Sandhoe House, on the Tyne, Residence of Sir Rowland Errington, Bart., 1850.

Alterations to the Rectory, Stockton-on-Tees, 1850.

Designed Residence for A. Topham Esq., Middlesbro, 1851.

Very large Additions to Residence of Robert Leadbitter, Esq., Ryton-on-Tyne, 1851.

*Designed High Cross, Benwell, 1851. (Now demolished).

Alterations to Newton Hall, Bywell-on-Tyne, Residence of W. Blackett, Esq., 1851.

Designed Residence of the Rev. Dr. Stephen Hawtrey, Near Windsor, 1851.

Designed *Oatlands House, Oatlands Park, Surrey, 1851.
(A Gabled Tudor Style Villa). Residence of William Chapman Hewitson, Esq., A well known Naturalist and friend of Dobson who bequeathed the house to John Hancock of Newcastle. (Demolished 1972).

*Large Additions to Sudbrooke Holme, Near Lincoln, Seat of Colonel Ellison, 1851. (Demolished)

Designed Dene House, Newcastle, Residence of Wm. Cruddace, Esq., 1851.

Designed Dildawn House, Kircudbrightshire, Residence of the Rev. Dr. Cowan, 1852.

Rebuilt and Enlarged the Leazes, Near Hexham Residence of William Kirsopp, Esq., 1853.

Designed Cleadon Meadows, Near Sunderland, Residence of Robert Shortridge, Esq., 1853.

Designed Inglethorpe Hall, Wisebech, Residence of Edward Metcalfe, Esq., 1854.

Designed Scar House, Arkendale, Yorkshire, Residence of J. Gilpin, Esq., 1855.

Alterations to Parsonage House, Seghill, 1855.

Large Additions to Holeyn Hall, Northumberland, Residence of J. James, Esq., 1858. (The Balustraded South Front is by Dobson and also the square balustraded Tower).

Additions to Shawdon, Northumberland, Residence of John Pawson, Esq., 1858.

Designed Banqueting Hall, Jesmond, Newcastle, for Sir William G. Armstrong, C.B., 1860. "a large rather dull Italianate apartment with statutary in niches"—Pevsner, p.257.

*Designed Greenwood, Hampshire, Residence of George Palmer, Esq., 1861.

Alterations to Wallington Hall, Northumberland, Seat of Sir Walter Trevelyan, Bart., 1855. (Executing Ruskin's suggestion of roofing-in the open courtyard and designing the arcaded walls and pillars for the paintings by William Bell Scott and others).

Alterations to Whitburn Hall, Near Sunderland, Residence of Sir Hedworth Williamson, Bart. (Now empty after conversion into flats. Application is now being made to demolish). 1856.

Designed Residences for James Morrison, Esq., Gresham Place, Newcastle; David Cram, Esq., Ellison Place, Newcastle; J. Harvey, Esq., Strawberry Place, Newcastle; William Todd, Esq., Picton Place, Newcastle; Dobson's own Residence 15 New Bridge Street, Newcastle (now embodied in a Dance Hall) and R. Plummer, Esq., Gateshead Fell.

Designed Lambton Castle, Durham Seat of the Earl of Durham, 1862. (Dobson died before the design could be implemented and the commission was completed by his son-in-law Sydney Smirke, RA).

ECCLESIASTICAL WORK

Designed New Road Chapel, Newcastle-on-Tyne, 1813.

Designed Scotch Church, North Shields, 1813.

Made designs of Tynemouth Priory, also a complete set of Drawings to show Restoration, 1813.

Prepared Plans for Restoring the Lady Chapel, Tynemouth, 1817. Not carried out until a date between 1843 and 1850.

Restored Hexham Abbey Church, 1817, 1818, 1852 and in 1858 rebuilt East end (Colvin, page 266) "In 1817 Dobson was called in by Colonel Beaumont to restore the East end of Hexham Abbey Church. Dobson urged that the East end, a fine example of the early pointed style, should be restored in harmony with the rest of the building, but his design was overruled and the Catherine wheel window of a late and debased style was consequently replaced. Dobson thirty years later demolished his own work and restored the harmony of the building by introducing two tiers of lancet windows similar to the Abbey Church in Whitby which Dobson considered of the same approximate date" – Newcastle Daily Chronicle 9th January 1865.

Restored St. John's Lee, Hexham (the East end rebuilt says Colvin p. 265). 1818.

Restoration at Gosforth Church, Newcastle. 1818.

Restoration at Whitburn Church, Near Sunderland, 1819.

Restorations at St. Mary's Church, Gateshead-on-Tyne, 1819-1855.

St. Nicholas' Church Newcastle-on-Tyne—Restored Steeple, 1819. Designed large Floral Gothic Window, North Transept, 1819. Tower foundations Restored 1832. Designed North and South Porches, 1832 (M. J. Dobson).

Some restorations at Whickham Church, Near Gateshead, 1819.

Commenced Design of St. Thomas' Church, Newcastle-on-Tyne, 1825. Consecrated 1830.

Restorations at Alnwick Church, Northumberland, 1825.

Designed Greenhead Church, Northumberland, 1826-1828. "The Dobson design has plain lancet windows and narrow West Tower with Spire", Pevsner, *Northumberland*, p. 160.

Designed *Presbyterian Chapel, Blackett Street, Newcastle-on-Tyne, (now demolished), 1826.

Designed Chancel of Belford Church, 1828.

Designed Chapel at Angerton House, Northumberland, 1828.

St. John's Church, Newcastle-on-Tyne, Restored Chancel & Gables, 1829. Restored West Side & Porch, 1848. Designed Altar Railing and Reredos, 1859. (M.J. Dobson).

Restoration at Hartburn Church, Northumberland, 1829.

Restoration at Stamfordham Church, Northumberland, 1830.

Designed Chancel to Dinnington Church, Northumberland, 1834.

Restored St. Edmund's Chapel, Gateshead-on-Tyne, 1836.

Designed Church at Warwick Bridge, Near Carlisle, for Peter Dixon, Esq., 1846.

Designed Jesmond Cemetery and Gates, Newcastle, 1839. The

Gates,—"Soberly classical with Doric Pilasters and two square Doric Turrets", J. C. Loudon said "The most appropriate cemetery lodge he knew"—quoted by Pevsner, p. 257. But Dobson designed also the whole interior lay-out and landscaped and planted it.

Designed St. Peter's *Newcastle-on-Tyne, 1839. Consecrated, 1843.

Restorations at Jarrow-on-Tyne, Church, 1840.

Designed Catholic Chapel at Horsley, Northumberland, 1841.

Designed Catholic Chapel, Felling, Gateshead-on-Tyne, 1841.

Designed Chapel, Priest's House, and Schools (Catholic), St. Mary and St. Joseph, at Birtley, Durham, 1842. Consecrated, 1844.

Designed Roman Catholic Chapel, for George Silvertopp, Esq., Minsteracres, Northumberland, 1843.

Restoration of St. Andrew's Church, Newcastle-on-Tyne. Restored South Transept, 1844; North Transept, 1845; Chancel, 1846. (M. J. Dobson).

Restored Oratory, Dungeon, and Keep, The Castle, Newcastle-on-Tyne, 1844.

Designed St. Cuthbert's, Bensham, 1844. Consecrated, 1846.

Designed Baptist Chapel, North Shields, 1845.

*Designed All Saints, Monkwearmouth, 1846.

Restorations at Alston Church, 1847.

Designed South Shields Presbyterian Church and Schools, Frederick Street, for J. Stevenson, Esq., 1847.

Re-designed St. Columba's Church, Stella, County Durham, 1848.

Restored Church at Winston, County Durham. 1848.

Designed Presbyterian Church, North Shields, 1856-7.

Restored Kirknewton Church, 1849, and also 1857.

Designed Benfieldside Church and Rectory, Shotley Bridge, 1849.

Restoration at Bywell St. Peter's Church, 1849.

St. Paul's Church and Rectory, Hendon, Near Sunderland, Designed 1850. Consecrated 1852.

Large Restorations at Lymm Church, Cheshire, 1850.

Restoration at Embleton Church, Northumberland, (including rebuilding of Craster Aisle—see Colvin p. 266), 1850.

Designed R.C. Church at Cowpen, Near Blyth, 1840.

*Designed Church of the Divine Unity, New Bridge Street, Newcastle, 1852. (Demolished).

*Designed Church of the Holy Trinity, New Bridge Street, Newcastle, 1847 (Demolished).

Restoration at Ford Church, 1852.

Restored Nave and Chancel of Chatton Church, Northumberland, 1853.

Bishopwearmouth Church. Restoration, 1849. Designed Rectory, 1853. Large Alterations to Church, 1853.

Designed Cemetery and Chapels, Hartlepool, 1855.

Designed Wesleyan Chapel, Howard Street, North Shields and St. Columba's Presbyterian Church, Northumberland Square, North Shields, 1856.

Designed Otterburn Church, Northumberland, 1858.

Designed Jesmond Parish Church (Clayton Memorial Church), Jesmond Road, Newcastle-on-Tyne, 1858. Consecrated 1861.

Restoration of great difficulty at St. Michael's Church, Houghton-le-Spring, County Durham, 1859. (In 1828 a tower with 6 bells was added weighing in all 1,500 tons thus causing pillars on NE and SE of Tower to shrink. Dobson took out the pillars and inserted new ones carrying the old mass of the masonry on wooden centres without settlement or collapse – M. J. Dobson's Memoir p. 43).

Restored Nave and Chancel of Warkworth Church, 1860.

Designed St. Mary's Church, Tyne Dock, 1861.

Designed St. Paul's, Elswick, Newcastle upon Tyne, 1861.

Designed Monument in Doncaster Church, to Memory of Miss Ellison, 1862.

Designed Sudbrooke Church, Sudbrooke Holme, near Lincoln, for Colonel Ellison, 1862.

SCHOOLS

Ponteland School, 1817.

Addition to Grammar School, Morpeth, 1827.

Hendon School, Near Sunderland, County Durham, 1831.

Chollerton School, 1831.

Stamfordham School, 1832.

School at Lymm, Cheshire, 1850.

Whixley School, Yorkshire, West Riding, 1853.

Bishopwearmouth School, near Sunderland, County Durham, 1853.

Ragged School, Newcastle-on-Tyne, 1853.

PUBLIC BUILDINGS AND STREETS

Alterations to Tynemouth House of Correction, 1814.

Alterations to Custom Houses at Liverpool, Glasgow and Newcastle, 1817.

Alterations to Old Theatre Royal Entrance, 1817.

Designed Morpeth Gaol, 1822.

*Designed Newcastle Gaol and House of Correction, Carliol Street, 1823. (Demolished)

Dobson's design for the New Centre of Newcastle involving purchase of 13 acres of Anderson Place, 1824. (Grainger in part adopted and varied this plan in 1831.

Designed *Eldon Square, including Northern Counties Club, 1824-33. (Demolished in the 1960's except for the East side).

Designed Lying-in Hospital, New Bridge Street, Newcastle, 1827. (Now BBC House, Newcastle).

Designed *Northern Academy of Art, 41 Blackett St., Newcastle, 1828. (Demolished 1974).

Designed Fish Market, Sandhill, Newcastle (by roofing over the former open columned Market at East end of Trollop's Guildhall), 1829.

Designed St. Mary's Place, Newcastle, 1829.

Designed *Royal Arcade, Newcastle, 1831-1832. (Demolished in 1963).

Designed Vegetable and Butcher Markets, 1834.

Designed elevations for East side of Grey Street, Newcastle, 1834-1837.

Designed Joint Stock Bank, Mosley Street, Newcastle, 1834.

Designed North Shields Town Hall, Northumberland, 1845.

Designed Surgeons Hall, Newcastle, Rye Hill, 1850.

Two Toll Houses: One near the new Dobson Infirmary Wing in Neville Street, and the other near St. Thomas's Church (see Colvin p. 264).

Designed Medical School, Newcastle, Neville Street, 1850-1851.

Designed Newcastle Central Railway Station, opened by Queen Victoria on 27th August 1850.

Designed New Wing Newcastle Infirmary, 1851.

Designed Warrington Museum and Library, Warrington, Lancashire, 1851.

Designed Baths and Terraces at Roker, 1855.

Designed Station Hotel, Leeds, 1857.

Designed Terraces, Crescent and an Hotel at West Cliff, Whitby, for George Hudson, MP for Sunderland, 1845-1857.

RAILWAYS, DOCKS AND INDUSTRIAL WORK

Planned Howdon-on-Tyne Docks, 1814.

Designed Warehouse at Broad Chare, Newcastle, 1814.

Designed Tyne Brewery, 1816.

Planned Blackburn's Docks, 1816.

Designed Glassworks, South Shields, for Mr. Cookson, 1817.

Designed Warehouses, Quayside, Newcastle for Mr. Sorsbie, 1818.

Designed Large Tobacco Warehouse, Quayside, Newcastle, 1819.

Planned new town of Seaham Harbour for Marquis of Londonderry, 1823. (Colvin states designs by Dobson are in the Durham County Record Office).

Designed Gateshead Railway Station, and Viaduct, 1841.

Designed Carlisle Railway Station, 1841.

Designed Monkwearmouth Docks (for George Hudson, MP), 1845.

Designed Manors Railway Station, Newcastle and Warehouses, 1850.

Designed Large Warehouses at Sunderland Docks, 1850.

Designed Warehouses at Liverpool, 1856.

BRIDGES

Designed Sandyford Bridge, Newcastle, 1818.

Designed Bridges for Newcastle and North Shields Railway, 1820.

Designed Bridges for Carlisle Railway, 1820.

Designed Hamsterley Bridge, 1825.

Designed Walbottle Bridge, 1827.

Designed Morpeth Bridge, 1830.

Designed Low Ford Bridge, near Morpeth, 1830.

Designed (with Robert Stephenson) High Level Bridge, Newcastle, 1846.

Designed Chatton Bridge, over the Fell, 1854.

MISCELLANEOUS WORK

Designed and Landscaped Artificial Lake at Bolam, Northumberland for Hon. Charles Beresford (later Lord Decies), 1818.

Designed Temple at Paine's Palladian Axwell Park, 1818.

Designed Collingwood Monument, Tynemouth, 1847.

Designed Freemason's Lodge, Middlesbrough, 1858.

ADDENDUM

Information as to the remodelling by Dobson in 1847 of the South elevation of Chollerton Vicarage (now Chollerton Grange) became known as this book went to press. Dobson also added two new rooms on the ground floor and two above. The plans for these alterations are in the County Record Office as part of the Newcastle Diocesan Records. *(Information by Roger Barnett, Esq. and Judge Denis Orde.)*

FOOTNOTES

1 *Country Life*, 5th Feb. 1976.

2 Bonomi designed with Wyatt the Palladian Wynyard Park for the Londonderry family and the Neo-classical Windlestone at Rushyford for the Edens.

3 In his Presidential address in 1859 to the newly formed Northern Architectural Association (See Appendix 1 to this book).

4 And the fine classical Church of St Anne's in City Road, Newcastle and Howick and North Dissington Halls.

5 Volume II, page 452.

6 Northumberland County Record Office ZM1/S52 and see Tyneside Classical (1964) by Wilkes and Dodds, page 32.

7 It has unfortunately been unlived in and unused for many years.

8 Presidential address, Northern Architectural Association 1898.

9 Quoted in "Palladio and English Palladianism" by Rudolf Wittkower at page 62 (Thames and Hudson 1974).

10 Sir Robert Smirke R.A. (1781-1867) Architect of Newton Don near Kelso, Roxburghshire, and many London buildings—Treasurer, Royal Academy, "Probably the most successful Architect of the early 19th Century"—Colvin.

11 Sydney Smirke R.A. (1798-1877) was more than Dobson's son-in-law. He became Dobson's best friend, his Executor, the man to whom he left his books and drawings, the man who generally accompanied him on his sketching tours in France and England and who received, with two of Dobson's children, and equal third share in his estate.

12 Printed as Appendix One to this book.

13 N. Pevsner, *Buildings of England; Northumberland* 1957, p. 252.

14 Designed as we have seen by Dobson's old master, David Stephenson, in the 1780s.

15 This is dealt with in detail in *Tyneside Classical* by Wilkes and Dodds (1964).

16 McKenzie's *History of Newcastle*, pages 199-203, Vol. 1.

17 Vol. 1, p. 200.

18 Demolished in 1963.

19 Demolished in the 1970s.

20 There is a famous painting by Henry Purlee Parker of this dinner in the Laing Art Gallery collection.

21 *Architectural and Picturesque views of Newcastle upon Tyne*, by Collard and Ross, 1842, (page 90).

22 Collard and Ross at page 91.

23 *The Buildings of Britain: Northumberland* 1957. p. 249.

24 Men of Mark TWIXT TYNE AND TWEED, Vol. II, p. 85.

25 See the article on Lilburn Tower by Gervase Jackson-Stops, Country Life, 8th November, 1973.

26 See Jackson-Stops articles on Beaufront Castle, County Life Feb. 5 & 12th 1976.

27 Country Life 8th November 1973.

28 A fine watercolour of the entrance tower of Mitford Manor by Like Clennel, a pupil of Thomas Bewick, hangs in the Laing Art Gallery, Newcastle upon Tyne.

29 *Country Life*, 17th February, 1966.

30 But at Beaufront and Lilburn the window is of stained glass designed and painted by William Wailes and commissioned specially for each house by Dobson.

31 G. Jackson-Stops on Lilburn Tower, *Country Life*, 8th November 1973.

32 Pevsner *op.cit.* p. 55, Penguin Books.

33 Reported in *The Yorkshire Gazette*, 6th January 1849.

34 It now hangs in the Committee Room of the Natural History Museum in Newcastle, a building designed by Wardle.

35 Pevsner calls it "one of the best in England"—*Northumberland*, p. 223.

36 Pages 50-51.

37 Colvin H. M. *A Biographical Dictionary of British Architects*, 2nd Edition, p. 263 (1978).

38 *Memoir*, p. 30.

39 *Memoir*, pp. 41-42.

40 Buildings of Northumberland p. 255 (Penguin Books).

41 From the University of Newcastle upon Tyne library. (Northern Architectural Association collection).

42 Document ZPE 59 Northumberland County Council Archives.

43 Kindly provided by Mr. Robin Gard, Northumberland County Archivist (SM1 B13 XII).

44 Quoted in *The Railway King* by Richard S. Lambert, pp. 64-65, 1934, Allen and Unwin.

45 The site plan made by Dobson in 1857 is with the Literary and Philosophical Society, Whitby.

46 In *A Survey of Whitby and the Surrounding Area*, edited by Professor G. H. J. Daysh, Shakespeare Head Press, Eton, Windsor, 1958.

47 *The Buildings of North Yorkshire*, p. 388, Penguin Books, 1966.

48 Now that it has been pulled down it would be interesting to have Dobson's views on the office block which has replaced it.

49 Quoted in Pevsner's *Northumberland* at page 257.

50 Throughout this list I have adhered to the county names and boundaries as they were in Dobson's time.